SUPER SUCKERS

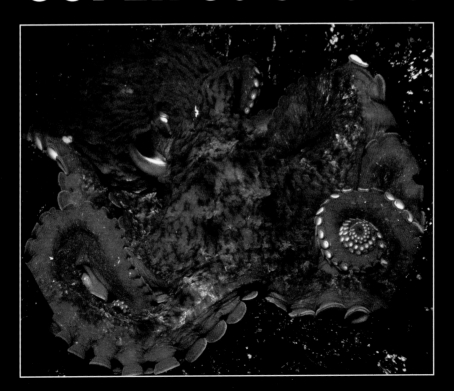

SUPER suckers

THE GIANT PACIFIC OCTOPUS

and Other Cephalopods
of the Pacific Coast

James A. Cosgrove
and
Neil McDaniel

HARBOUR PUBLISHING

Harbour Publishing Co. Ltd.
P.O. Box 219, Madeira Park, BC, V0N 2H0
www.harbourpublishing.com

Image credits: Front cover, giant Pacific octopus by David Fleetham. Page 1, giant Pacific octopus by Neil McDaniel. Pages 2–3, *King of the Kelp Forest* watercolour by Mark Hobson. Page 5, giant Pacific octopus interacting with diver by David Fleetham. Pages 6–7, giant Pacific octopus gliding by Neil McDaniel. Back cover, top, hatching giant Pacific octopuses by Fred Bavendam; middle, octopus eye by Neil McDaniel; bottom, opalescent squid by Neil McDaniel.

Text design and layout by Martin Nichols
Printed in Canada
Printed on paper containing 10% post-consumer fibre

BRITISH
COLUMBIA
ARTS COUNCIL
Supported by the Province of British Columbia

THE CANADA COUNCIL | LE CONSEIL DES ARTS
FOR THE ARTS | DU CANADA
SINCE 1957 | DEPUIS 1957

Harbour Publishing acknowledges financial support from the Government of Canada through the Book Publishing Industry Development Program and the Canada Council for the Arts, and from the Province of British Columbia through the BC Arts Council and the Book Publishing Tax Credit.

Library and Archives Canada Cataloguing in Publication

Cosgrove, James Albert, 1945–

Super suckers : the giant Pacific octopus and other cephalopods of the Pacific coast / Jim Cosgrove, Neil McDaniel.

Includes bibliographical references and index.
ISBN 978-1-55017-466-3

1. North Pacific giant octopus. 2. Octopuses—Northwest Coast of North America. 3. Squids—Northwest Coast of North America. I. McDaniel, Neil, 1949– II. Title.

QL430.3.O2C67 2009594'.56C2008-907919-1

JAC dedicates this book to his wife Jeannie
and daughter Jillian.

NM dedicates this book to his wife Tenny
and daughters Elisabeth and Cathryn.

Table of Contents

Introduction

"Supple as leather, tough as steel, cold as night!" That horrific description of the arms of an octopus was penned by Victor Hugo in his 1866 novel *Les Travailleurs de la Mer (Toilers of the Sea)*, which recounts the dramatic account of a fight to the death between the hero, Gilliatt, and a fearsome octopus. Since then, the reputation of these eight-armed cephalopods has improved somewhat, although as late as the 1960s, neoprene-suited divers in British Columbia and Washington engaged in popular octopus wrestling contests, each frogman vying to surface with the biggest octopus.

While no longer considered evil, the cunning devilfish—the giant Pacific octopus—remains an enigmatic creature. It reaches prodigious size, is a master of disguise and is immensely strong when fully mature. It grows more swiftly than nearly any other marine animal yet lives only a few short years. Superbly mobile, it can stroll over the bottom in a graceful eight-legged shuffle or abruptly launch into jet-propulsion mode, blasting water through its funnel to disappear in a billowing cloud of brown ink.

All of these characteristics are impressive in themselves, but it is the apparent intelligence of this animal that is most intriguing. It amazes us with behaviours that belie its status as a lowly invertebrate (an animal entirely lacking a backbone). We now realize that it is capable of learning from previous experiences and possesses some form of memory, at least in the short term. Some divers have even established associations with particular octopuses, animals that willingly leave the protection of their dens to interact with bubble-blowing visitors.

In this book we examine all aspects of the lives of these fascinating cephalopods. Included are many insights derived from Jim's 40 years of undersea observations and original research. Some of the extraordinary behaviours and new aspects of biology that they present have not been described before. Neil seldom

On the move and alert for prey, a giant Pacific octopus strides over a sandy bottom. Photo Neil McDaniel

ventures below the surface without a camera, and the octopus is one of his favourite subjects.

This book also presents the personal observations and often humorous anecdotes of researchers, aquarists and veteran divers who have witnessed the sometimes baffling, always remarkable behaviours of the giant Pacific octopus.

We describe the natural history of some other interesting cephalopods found along the northeast Pacific coast, too, including the Pacific red octopus, smoothskin octopus, opalescent squid, stubby squid, Humboldt squid, neon flying squid, North Pacific giant squid and giant squid. But our great interest and our primary subject is the giant Pacific octopus.

—Jim Cosgrove and Neil McDaniel

The Stuff of Myths and Movies

Consider the octopus. Is there a more bizarre-looking, homely animal in the sea? A baggy, sac-like body surmounted by a pair of bulging, slitted eyes and fleshy horns. Eight snake-like arms studded with hundreds of grasping suction cups. A stubby funnel projecting from its body like a leftover piece of fire hose. Surely the word cuddly doesn't spring to mind when contemplating these slithery creatures.

Its unattractive appearance hasn't done its reputation any favours. Throughout history many malicious characteristics have been attributed to this mild-mannered mollusc, mostly without justification. Native cultures throughout the world have traditional histories that cast the octopus as a devil or in an evil role, and it is referred to as a devilfish or demon in the languages of many societies. Even now it is often fascination dusted with a pinch of fear that compels people to watch an octopus on TV or in an aquarium. To this day some people find this creature extremely repulsive.

• •

Opposite: A mask created by Glen Rabena portrays the octopus in First Nations art. Born in Washington state, Glen was adopted into the Eagle Clan by hereditary Haida chief Claude Davidson. Photo Anne Sheridan

Extraordinary in form and behaviour, the enigmatic octopus has featured prominently in the oral myths and legends of native cultures, the writings of naturalists and novelists and the imaginations of film producers.

FIRST NATIONS LEGENDS

First Nations lore often portrays the octopus as a servant or a powerful sea-spirit helper to the chief of the undersea world. It is sometimes depicted as a monster that can devour canoes and even whole villages.

The octopus features in the art of healers, probably due to its ability to change colour and texture and regenerate tissue. The octopus is part of the crest of the Tsimshian Eagle clan. The Haida and Nuu-chah-nulth Nations also depict the octopus in their myths and legends.

To the Kwakwaka'wakw Nation the octopus is a symbol of wealth. The number eight is considered magical, and this adds to the mystique of the octopus.

"The Legend of Mr. Raven and Miss Octopus" appears in *Teachings of the Tides: Uses of Marine Invertebrates by the Manhousat People*, by David Ellis and Luke Swan:

> One lovely morning the tide was going out. The older people, as they often did, came out of the house early. Before having breakfast they came out and sat down at their nawaayas (daily sitting place). They told each other many stories.

Opposite top: Carved from western red cedar, this octopus mask was created by Bill Henderson of the Kwakwaka'wakw in 1980.
Courtesy Royal BC Museum, Image 16780

Opposite bottom: A stylized octopus silkscreen print, created by Mark Henderson of the Kwakwaka'wakw in 1981.
Courtesy Royal BC Museum, Image 17233

When the tide had gone out far enough the old people saw a lady with long braided hair walk down the beach. Her hair hung down as far as her hips. She had a digging stick in her hand and a basket on her back. She was Tiilhuupas, Miss Octopus, the lady with the long hair.

"I think she is going to dig clams," said one of the old people. Miss Octopus sat down on a rock so she wouldn't get wet. The tide was still going out and the gravel was wet. She sat there and started to dig for clams with her yew wood digging stick. She dug one clam and threw it into her basket.

Then a man came out of one of the houses. He walked down the beach toward Miss Octopus.

"Oh look at Mr. Raven, he is going down to the beach, look at him! He is going to do something. Yes, he is up to something, because he has seen the young lady down there digging clams. You just watch him now," said one of the old people. Mr. Raven went close to the lady.

"Lady, you are digging clams, aren't you?" he asked. She didn't even shake her head to answer him. She kept digging and didn't pay attention to him. Miss Octopus didn't like him at all. And after a while, Mr. Raven said the same thing, "Digging clams Miss Octopus?" His voice was different from the way he usually spoke; it had a strange tone to it. Miss Octopus kept digging. In the back of her mind, she was thinking of what she would do when the tide started to come in again. If Mr. Raven kept asking the same question she was going to have to do something about him.

"Are you digging clams Miss Octopus?" he said again. The tide turned and started to flow back in. It was getting closer to where she was digging. "Are you digging clams?" Mr. Raven asked again. Finally the water reached the hole where Miss Octopus was digging and it flowed in. Then she dropped her digging stick and grabbed Mr. Raven.

"Yes, Mr. Raven, I am digging clams," she said. That long hair of hers had become arms, eight arms. She had put some of her arms around Mr. Raven. "Yes, Mr. Raven, I am digging clams. You asked me that and now I am going to answer you—I am digging clams. I have my children to feed. Clams are the only food that we eat. Yes I am digging clams!" Both of them stood up.

"Oh please, oh please Miss Octopus, let me go," begged Mr. Raven.

"You were asking me if I was digging clams. I was digging clams. You can hear now that I am digging clams." She kept holding on to him. The tide had come in up to their waists.

"Now let me go, please let me go," he pleaded again. The water went up to their shoulders.

"You were asking me if I was digging clams. Now I am going to answer your question. I was digging clams." The water went up to their necks.

"Please let me go! It's up to my neck now!" pleaded Mr. Raven.

"I was digging clams, Mr. Raven, I was digging clams." Finally the tide flowed in over their heads.

And one of the old people said, "Look at Mr. Raven. You heard what he was saying, and now she is answering him. She won't let him go. Of course he was bothering her when she was digging clams. Now she is answering him; she is going to hold on to him." The old people started to laugh.

It didn't take long for Mr. Raven to run out of breath and drown. Then Miss Octopus let go of his body and it rose to the surface. But Miss Octopus was used to the

Artwork by Patrick Amos illustrates the First Nations legend of Mr. Raven and Miss Octopus. Photo Jim Cosgrove

salt water; she could live underwater for many hours. Mr. Raven floated belly up, with his legs stiffened. He was dead. His body drifted ashore. And one of the old people said, "Now some of you people, you go and see Miss Crow, who is the cousin of Mr. Raven, and tell her what has happened. And then you can all help to take his body and put it away. But you know how Mr. Raven is; he will be up and around again tomorrow, for he knows how to make himself come alive again."

So the people helped Miss Crow put the body away. Of course, the next day Mr. Raven was alive again.

The story teaches the Manhousat people never to have anything to do with a live octopus, or they could be held down and end up like Mr. Raven.

EIGHT-ARMED DEMONS

The octopus appears prominently in literature throughout the ages, no doubt due to its strange appearance and fabled strength. Only a few scribes approach the subject with anything but a narrow-minded view, and the octopus's reputation has taken an undeserved beating.

Early writers have plenty to say, none of it flattering. Around AD 77 Pliny the Elder, in his comprehensive encyclopedia of the natural world, *Naturalis Historia*, has these unkind words about the octopus:

> *"No animal is more savage in causing the death of man in the water; for it struggles with him by coiling round him and it swallows him with sucker-cups and drags him asunder by its multiple suction, when it attacks men who have been shipwrecked or are diving."*

Tales of ships being attacked and sunk by monstrous cephalopods inspired illustrations by artists who embellished their work considerably. This one is enough to put you off boating forever!
Hart Nautical Collections, MIT Museum

If that lurid description seems over the top, it fairly pales in comparison to the treatment our eight-armed innocent receives from the pen of the French writer Victor Hugo. Hugo's 1866 novel *Toilers of the Sea* contained a exciting account of the hero Gilliatt's battle with a giant octopus. The tone is nearly hysterical:

> *"It is with the sucking apparatus that it attacks. The victim is oppressed by a vacuum drawing at numberless points; it is not a clawing or a biting, but an indescribable scarification. A tearing of the flesh is terrible, but less terrible than a sucking of the blood. Claws are harmless compared with the horrible action of these natural air-cups. The talons of the wild beast will enter your flesh; but with the cephaloptera [sic] it is you who enter into the creature. The muscles swell, the fibres of the body are contorted, the skin cracks under the loathsome oppression, the blood spurts out and mingles horribly with the lymph of the monster, which clings to its victim by innumerable hideous mouths. The hydra incorporates itself with the man; the man becomes one with the hydra. The spectre lies upon you; the tiger can only devour you; the devil-fish, horrible, sucks your life blood away."*

One might think that, as we got to know these elusive animals a little better, their reputation would improve. That did occur to some extent as more rational authors gave the octopus credit for some praiseworthy characteristics. But much of the literature continues the character assassination. Consider this description by inventor, photographer and filmmaker John Williamson in his 1936 autobiographical book *Twenty Years Under the Sea*:

> *"I have seen many of these horrible creatures during my twenty years under the sea. Filled with a strange fascination, combined with indescribable loathing, I have watched these devils of the sea in their native haunts. I have seen them seize, kill and devour their prey, and although safely ensconced behind the thick*

*glass of my window, I have never been able to over-
come a feeling of dread, of instinctive fear, at the sight
of these eight-armed demons. A man-eating shark, a
giant poison-fanged moray, a murderous barracuda,
appear harmless, innocent, friendly and even attrac-
tive when compared to the octopus. No words can ad-
equately describe the sickening horror one feels when
from some dark mysterious lair, the great lidless eyes
stare at one. People speak of the cold eyes of fishes, of
the cruel, baleful eyes of sharks, but in all creation
there are no eyes like those of the octopus. They are
everything that is horrible. Dead eyes. The eyes of a
corpse through which the demon peers forth, unearthly,
expressionless, yet filled with such bestial malignancy
that one's very soul seems to shrink beneath their gaze,
and cold perspiration beads the brow."*

All this bluster from a man sitting fairly comfortably inside his
photoscope, a spherical observation chamber he designed to enable subsea photography. What about the vulnerable hard-hat
divers who were actually immersed in the same ocean as these
demons? Lt. Commander G. Williams, author of the 1926 book
Diving for Treasure and Other Adventures Beneath the Sea, wrote:

*"Perhaps the most dangerous fish of all is the octopus
...From what I have seen, it is as cruel as it is greedy,
for it kills for the mere sake of killing...If a diver is attacked by one of these creatures it is only by superhu-
man efforts that he can free himself from its terrible
grasp. There are cases on record when the struggle has
only been terminated when the diver and his adver-
sary have been hauled bodily to the surface and on to
the deck of the diving vessel, and even then the octopus
has fought furiously to the last gasp."*

Opposite: In Victor Hugo's *Toilers of the Sea*, first published in Paris
in 1866, the hero Gilliatt battles a monstrous octopus to the death.
Mariners' Museum, Newport News, Virginia

Trust the eloquent Jacques Cousteau to finally paint the octopus in a favourable light. In the 1978 book Octopus and Squid: The Soft Intelligence, he and co-author Philippe Diole express their admiration:

"One must have lived in the water with octopuses for months, swum in the same waters, brushed past the same algae in order to be able to appreciate the beauty of the octopus. In the water, the octopus looks like a silken scarf floating, swirling, and settling gently as a leaf on a rock, the color of which it immediately assumes. Then it disappears into a crack which appears to be hardly large enough to accommodate one of its arms, let alone its entire body. The whole process is reminiscent of a ballet. It is somehow ethereal and, at the same time, elaborate, elegant and slightly mischievous."

STARS OF THE SILVER SCREEN

While the great white shark of *Jaws* set the bar sky-high for on-screen terror—"You're gonna need a bigger boat!"—giant deep-sea squids and monstrous octopuses have had their fair share of movie infamy. Squids and octopuses lack the blood-spilling dentition of sharks, but their sinuous multi-suckered arms and razor-sharp beaks have made them suitable subjects of terror in Hollywood's B movies.

Giant octopuses have starred in numerous film productions. They've been chillingly portrayed as monstrous, savage killers lusting for the chance to attack an unwary diver, a ship or even an entire coastal city. Long before giant man-eating sharks began ravaging coastal New England, giant octopuses were the villains of choice in cheesy horror flicks.

The giant octopus made its first film appearance in 1916 in *20,000 Leagues under the Sea*. It was produced by John Williamson, who had taken the first underwater pictures in North America. His father had invented a deep-sea tube, made of a series of concentric interlocking rings that stretched like an accordion.

Suspended from a ship it enabled observation and filming at considerable depth.

In his fascinating 2006 book *Monsters of the Sea,* Richard Ellis describes how the ingenious Williamson made the movie:

"Although the *Nautilus* is attacked by a giant squid in the novel, Williamson substituted an octopus, which attacks a diver instead of the submarine. When Nemo sees the diver in trouble, he quickly dons his diving apparatus, descends on the submarine's retractable ladder, and confronts the monster. From his own book, *Twenty Years Under the Sea,* John Williamson narrates the encounter: 'Into the field of vision came the grotesque figure of the helmeted diver, the gallant Captain Nemo. How slowly, how very deliberately he seemed to move. Moments dragged in tense suspense. Now he was beside the native who was struggling in the clutches of the squirming python-like tentacle. A flash of his broad-bladed axe—the tentacle fell—and the struggling native shot to the surface, gasping for breath but saved!'

"According to Williamson, people believed the encounter was genuine. He quotes a review from the Philadelphia *Public Ledger* that said: 'The struggle between the monstrous cephalopod and the pearl diver, ending in the latter's rescue by the captain, is one of the rarities of the camera. There can be no question of fake or

THE NAME GAME

The scientific name for the giant Pacific octopus has changed many times since it was first described in 1862, as cephalopod taxonomists (those who study the relationships between organisms) have made revisions to reflect changing judgments. In 1998 the scientific name *Enteroctopus dofleini* (Wülker, 1910) was adopted, but prior to that it has been known as:

Octopus dofleini martini Pickford, 1964
Paroctopus asper Akimushkin, 1963
Octopus madokai Berry, 1921
Octopus apollyon Berry, 1913
Octopus dofleini apollyon (Berry, 1912)
Polypus apollyon (Berry, 1912)
Octopus dofleini dofleini (Wülker, 1910)
Octopus hongkongensis Hoyle, 1885
Octopus punctatus Gabb, 1862

deception. It is all there, and our vision tells us it is all true.' In fact, it was one of the first 'special effects' in movie history, and the only part that was 'true' was the diver. Williamson had designed a giant octopus made of canvas with halved rubber balls sewn into the arms to represent suckers. The tentacles were spring-loaded contraptions inflated with rubber tubing that could be activated by bursts of compressed air to give them the appearance of life. The octopus machine (which Williamson patented) was controlled by a diver inside the head, and the inventor felt very proud indeed of the lifelike appearance of his octopus. He wrote: 'To one who did not know its inner secrets, viewing it in action was indeed a hair-raising experience. John Barrymore himself told me that in all his career on the stage and screen he had never been so thrilled, so absolutely frozen—rooted to the spot—as when he watched my octopus scenes.'"

The special effects in the 1937 black and white production *Killers of the Sea*, directed by Raymond Friedgen, were considerably less ambitious. Scenes of rather puny octopuses in an aquarium were intercut with those of a helmeted diver stomping over the bottom. The narration, however, more than compensated for the modest visuals. How's this for breathless prose?

> *"The octopus glides, sinuous, sinister, like a horrible symbol of sin. The octopus, the devilfish—slimy, slithery, hateful—a loathsome nightmare that lurks with hideous peril for the diver! It has eight arms, snaky tentacles, each with a row of suckers that cling with a deadly clutch, the dread of every diver. Its bite is murderous, its saliva poisonous, and it grows to enormous size—sometimes an arm spread of 128 feet—so diver beware! The octopus—the lore of the sea is full of its terror with its attacks upon human beings and its unmitigated ferocity! The octopus is so fierce that the devilfish when hungry has been known to attack one of its own tentacles and devour its own arms!"*

"An arm spread of 128 feet" (39 m) might seem just a tad hyperbolic, but in *It Came from Beneath the Sea*, released by

Columbia Pictures in 1955, the eight-armed menace was bigger still. The plot concerns a wacky octopus that has become radio-active due to an atomic bomb test. The radiation apparently scrambles its brain, because it inexplicably decides that fishes are no longer satisfactory food and engages in a series of frenzied attacks on man-made artifacts. Ships, railway cars, police vehicles and ultimately the Golden Gate Bridge are demolished by this crazed cephalopod.

In 1977 Italian filmmakers had a go at riding the bloody coat-tails of *Jaws*, which had been released two years earlier, with the production of *Tentacoli* (*Tentacles*). They engaged a star-studded cast that included Henry Fonda, John Huston, Shelley Winters, Claude Akins and Bo Hopkins (none of whom, it seems, took the time to actually read the script before they signed on). It was an unmitigated disaster. Richard Ellis, in *Monsters of the Sea*, surveys the wreckage:

"As in *Jaws*, various people are picked off by an unknown creature, but there the resemblance ends. *Tentacles* is a witless

WHAT DO YOU CALL MORE THAN ONE?

One of the ongoing debates is on the question of whether more than one octopus should be called octopi, octopuses or octopodes. In scientific terms one octopus is an octopod, derived from a Greek word. The plural of some Greek words is made by adding "-es," which would make the plural "octopodes." This plural is common in European literature. North Americans somehow decided that octopus was a Latin word, as many scientific words are, and added an "i" to form the Latin plural "octopi." This is incorrect but still commonly found in newspapers and popular magazines. Somehow North Americans are still not able to agree that the Europeans have it right, so now we have settled on calling multiple animals "octopuses." Who are we to thwart convention? We use "octopuses" as the plural in this book and note that many Europeans now use this form too.

hodge-podge of jiggling cameras, befuddled editing, missed (and occasionally dubbed) lines, and utter plotlessness. The story—what little there is of it—has something to do with use of 'illegal' high-frequency sounds that entice some sort of sea creature to go on a rampage, so we see people yanked underwater or simply disappearing, that being easier and cheaper than trying to make an octopus. Every once in a while there is a murky shot of a real octopus in a tank, accompanied by ghastly tweeting noises, but otherwise the monster never appears."

In the 1978 science fiction production *Warlords of Atlantis,* the plot concerns a voyage to the lost world of Atlantis. A gigantic octopus attacks the ship *Texas Rose* and kidnaps the crew, then retreats to its cave. Richard Ellis assesses the talent:

"As cinematic model octopuses go, this is a pretty good specimen. The first time we see it, it is swimming past the bathy-sphere, with its writhing arms spread wide, but when it surfaces, its head looks surprisingly real. The attack, with the arms squirming down the stairwells and through the portholes to grab the sailors, is a bad version of a similar scene in the Disney *20,000 Leagues Under the Sea,* but not nearly as well done, since wires employed to move the arms are often clearly visible. We see the octopus's wrinkled, mottled head, and sometimes its staring yellow eye, which has a correctly horizontal pupil. When the makers of *Warlords of Atlantis* wanted a monster that could inspire terror in the eyes of men, seek vengeance for stolen property, and grab several sailors at the same time as it smashes up a ship with a golden idol, which one did they choose? The giant octopus, of course."

Thankfully, a number of excellent documentary films have provided entertaining and factual depictions of the octopus. One of the best is the 1966 film *Octopus & Squid: Incredible Suckers,* part of the BBC Natural History Unit's award-winning series *World of Wildlife.* Narrated by Sir David Attenborough, filmed and hosted by Mike deGruy, it provides a fascinating look at many cephalopods, including the giant Pacific octopus.

About the Molluscs

The giant Pacific octopus is a member of the phylum Mollusca (alternatively spelled Molluska), a very successful group of invertebrate animals that includes more than 46,000 marine, freshwater and terrestrial species. Included in this diverse assemblage are many familiar animals with external shells such as mussels, chitons, snails, clams and scallops; those with reduced internal shells such as the cuttlefishes and squids; and some that lack shells altogether, such as the octopuses and sea slugs.

Features common to nearly all molluscs include a bilaterally symmetrical body—in other words, the left side is a mirror image of the right side—with a head, muscular foot and a visceral mass that contains the internal organs. The mantle, a sheet of skin and muscle extending from the body wall, covers all or part of the body. Inside the mantle cavity lie the gills and the openings for the excretory and reproductive systems. In many molluscs the mantle secretes a calcareous shell into which the animal can retract for protection, but in some groups the shell is internal or missing entirely. One structure unique to this phylum is the radula, a file-like, toothed organ in the mouth that can drill holes or shred prey.

There are seven major classes within the phylum Mollusca. The best known are the Polyplacophora (chitons), the Gastropoda (snails and nudibranchs), the Bivalvia (clams, mussels, oysters and scallops) and the Cephalopoda (squids, cuttlefishes and octopuses).

The cephalopods are the most highly developed class of molluscs. Included are tiny species of octopus no bigger than a fingertip and monstrous deep-sea squids 14 m (46 ft) long. At any size, cephalopods share common traits such as bilateral symmetry, a shell gland, a mantle and a well-developed head with arms bearing suckers. In the centre of the arms is the mouth, containing a horny, parrot-like beak and a radula.

The senses of sight and taste, with advanced eyes that are nearly as complex as our own and suckers that can taste, are extremely acute. Cephalopods have no ears or voice box, so they cannot hear or vocalize.

Above: Bivalve molluscs have a pair of rigid calcareous shells to protect their internal organs. The weathervane scallop (*Patinopectin caurinus*) lives on deeper sandy bottoms. Photo Neil McDaniel

Opposite: An encounter with an octopus is always a thrill.
Photo Brandon Cole

Opposite top left: In nudibranchs (sea slugs), the molluscan shell has been lost altogether, and the animals are apparently defenceless. Many have toxic flesh, however, and some loudly advertise this fact with bold colours and patterns. The name nudibranch means "naked gills"; the pointed structures visible on the alabaster nudibranch (*Dirona albolineata*) are its external gills. Photo Neil McDaniel

Opposite top right: Chitons are bottom-dwelling molluscs with eight shell plates surrounded by a fleshy girdle. *Tonicella lineata,* a herbivore, scrapes algae from rocks with its toothed radula. Photo Neil McDaniel

Opposite bottom left: Bivalves such as oysters, clams, mussels and scallops also are related to the cephalopods. The swimming scallop (*Chlamys* species) is commonly found in current-swept areas where it feeds on plankton. The sponge that inhabits the valves of the scallop may provide protection from attacks by sea stars, crabs and even giant Pacific octopuses due to its unpleasant taste and texture. Photo Neil McDaniel

Opposite bottom right: Snails—univalve molluscs—provide food for humans, and their shells are highly prized as examples of nature's art. One of the West Coast's most colourful species is the painted top snail (*Calliostoma annulatum*). Photo Neil McDaniel

Most cephalopods breathe by drawing water into the mantle cavity through gill slits on either side of the head. When these slots are sealed by muscular contractions, the animals can forcefully eject water through a hose-like funnel called the siphon. This enables them to swim rapidly using water jet propulsion. Some cephalopods also have an ink sac that empties into the mantle cavity near the funnel. When the animals flee a predator, they can discharge the ink, creating a smoke screen that may confuse the attacker.

Most cephalopods have special pigment cells in their skin that enable them to camouflage themselves or to signal others.

Cephalopods have separate sexes. Elaborate courtship rituals often precede mating; during both rituals and mating, the sexes may display various colours and patterns. In most cephalopods one of the male's arms—the hectocotylus—is specially modified for transferring sperm packets to the female. The females lay eggs that develop directly into juveniles (called paralarvae) that are almost identical to the adult. Most octopus females

stay with their eggs and brood them until they hatch. Squids and cuttlefishes generally lay their eggs, leave and die shortly afterward.

Cephalopods live in all the world's oceans, from the intertidal zone to abyssal depths. Squids often form huge schools, free-swimming together in open water. On the other hand, most octopuses are solitary creatures that live on the bottom, often in coral or rocky dens.

Active and usually swift predators, cephalopods eat a wide variety of invertebrates and fishes. In turn they are eaten by larger fishes and mammals including, of course, humans.

Above: Capable of remarkably complex signalling displays, Caribbean reef squids (*Sepioteuthis sepioidea*) are fascinating to watch in warm tropical waters. Photo Neil McDaniel

Right: The most ancient of the modern cephalopods is the chambered nautilus (*Nautilus* species). Living in the South Pacific, this cephalopod group—represented by only six species—is the only one to have an external shell. Photo Brandon Cole

Top: The Caribbean reef octopus (*Octopus briareus*) is active and aggressive at night. It pounces over coral heads with arms spread wide, capturing crustaceans and fish snared by the suckers and parachute-like web.
Photo Neil McDaniel

Bottom: Seen at night in Hawaiian waters where the coral reef ends and the sandy drop-off begins, this species has remarkably long, snake-like arms. It is known as the ornate or night octopus, *Octopus ornatus*.
Photo David Fleetham

Two male giant Australian cuttlefishes (*Sepia apama*) engage in some dramatic posturing, possibly for the benefit of a female. Cuttlefishes often live less than one year, and the buoyant cuttlebone (skeletal support) may drift to the beach when a cuttlefish dies. Photo Brandon Cole

The class Cephalopoda, which includes approximately 600 living species, has two subclasses. The Nautiloidea (chambered nautiluses) have a coiled, many-chambered external shell and 90 or more suckerless tentacles. The Coleoidea (squids, cuttlefishes and octopuses), whose shells are internal or absent, have eight to 10 appendages, highly developed eyes, an ink sac and pigment cells in the skin.

Within the Coleoidea, the order Sepioidea contains the cuttlefishes and bobtailed squids. These are extremely mobile and

have an internal calcareous shell, a short body with lateral fins, eight arms plus two specialized tentacles used for capturing prey, and special skin cells that enable a remarkable repertoire of signalling colours and patterns.

The order Teuthoidea comprises the squids. These animals have an internal horny rod called a pen. The body is torpedo-shaped with lateral fins, and many species are capable of very speedy swimming. They have eight arms and two extensible tentacles that are especially adept at catching prey. Some species rank

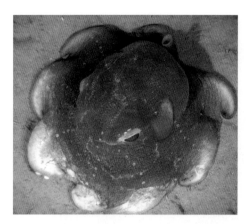

Commonly called the Dumbo octopus after the Walt Disney animation, this deep-water specimen (*Opisthoteuthis californiana*) is one of the cirrate or finned octopuses. It was photographed by the ROPOS Remotely Operated Vehicle within the Olympic Coast National Marine Sanctuary off the west coast of Washington at a depth of 332 m (1,090 ft). Courtesy Olympic Coast National Marine Sanctuary

as the fastest swimmers in the ocean and are among the largest of all living invertebrates.

The order Vampyromorpha is represented worldwide by the single species *Vampyroteuthis infernalis*. These small cephalopods have eight long arms and two thread-like filaments in pits between the first two pairs of arms. Their eight arms are joined by an umbrella-like, delicate web of skin that is used to trap prey. Their eyes are huge for their overall size, and they have light-producing organs in their skin and produce a glowing cloud of ink. Rarely seen alive, they live in deep water down to 900 metres (3,000 ft).

The order Octopoda contains the octopuses, which are further divided into suborders based on the presence or absence of fins. The Cirrata are deep-sea octopuses that usually have fins. They are rarely seen alive except from deep-diving submersibles, generally below 2,000 m (6,600 ft). Suborder Incirrata contains familiar octopuses—including the giant Pacific octopus—which do not have fins.

EVOLUTION

To appreciate some of the incredible forms that cephalopods have taken over time, we must look back to their beginnings more than half a billion years ago. We are extremely fortunate that many of the ancient cephalopods had hard shells that were preserved as fossils.

Cephalopod evolution, it is important to understand, has not been a linear process with one group leading directly to future groups. Over time many groups were unsuccessful dead-ends. Three anatomically and ecologically different groups each evolved independently of the others and experienced different successes and failures. The three groups are the subclasses Nautiloidea, Ammonoidea and Coleoidea.

The earliest fossils of cephalopods were the ancestors of the nautilus, and lived about 550 million years ago (mya). The first cephalopod was an animal called *Plectronoceras*. This is known from some two-centimetre (0.8 in) broken shells found in northeast China. These shells, however, show many features found in a modern nautilus such as having a tightly coiled shell with gas chambers. These very early cephalopods survived for millions of years, diversifying into four orders, but almost became extinct between 500 and 430 mya. Only one of the orders survived, but it flourished and came to occupy much more of the world; its fossils are now found in China, Europe and North America. The ancestor of the modern nautilus is found in the fossil record about 215 mya. All of the other nautiloid lines died out to leave only the modern nautilus, within a single family, two genera and five species.

The ammonites arose and rapidly diversified during the period between 400 and 65 mya. Their shells generally became longer,

Life in an ancient ocean is the subject of a diorama at the Smithsonian National Museum of Natural History in Washington, DC. Cephalopods were major predators as well as prey for some of the even larger vertebrates alive at that time. Ammonites, among the most common of the cephalopods, had variously shaped shells. Photo Jim Cosgrove

with lengths up to 10 m (33 ft). In some cases the shells evolved to become straighter, while in others they became tightly coiled.

Some of the shells developed complex internal systems of tubes and coils. Externally the shells ranged from smooth to very ornate with ridges and grooves. It is speculated that this great diversity was due in part to the predators that the cephalopods had to contend with. This same process can be seen today in a marine snail called the dog whelk (*Nucella lamellosa*), which has a smooth shell in habitats where there are no crabs and a very thick, convoluted shell where crabs are a major predator. Although success-ful for over 300 million years, the ammonites disappeared from the fossil record at the same time the dinosaurs went extinct. There are no living ammonites.

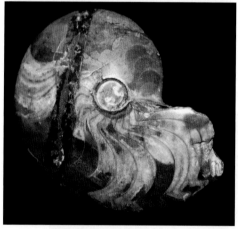

The fossil group most suc-cessful into the modern era

Top: The ammonite depicted in this display at the Smithsonian National Museum of Natural History in Washington, DC, is one of the elongate or straight forms. These animals and their kin prowled the oceans for several hundred million years. Photo Jim Cosgrove

Bottom: Ammonites were among the most successful and diverse groups of ancestral cephalopods. Their external shells ranged from straight to tightly coiled and from plain to very ornate. Size ranged from a few centi-metres to more than 10 m (33 feet), and weights were into the hundreds of kilograms. The ammonites became extinct about 65 million years ago. Photo Jim Cosgrove

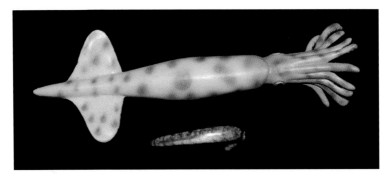

Dating back almost half a billion years, the belemnites are an ancestral form of the cephalopod line. Now extinct, members of this diverse group are only known from fossils of their internal shells (fossil below model). This model shows how a belemnite was thought to have looked, although the skin colour and texture are guesswork. Photo Jim Cosgrove

is the subclass Coleoidea, which has given rise to the modern cuttlefishes, squids and octopuses. The coleoides appeared in the fossil record about the same time as the ammonites and evolved along with the ammonites, but some were able to survive the great extinction that occurred 65 mya. The belemnites—a group of coleoides that looked somewhat squid-like with paired fins but that also had an internal chambered shell like that of the nautiloids—were very successful but became extinct at the same time as the ammonites.

With the disappearance of the ammonites, the coleoides had new ecological niches available to them and evolved to fill those niches. At this point the evolutionary ancestry becomes much more difficult to trace, as the squids have a softer internal skeleton (the pen), and the octopuses have lost their shell completely. As soft tissues seldom fossilize, it is difficult for scientists to determine exact relationships of cephalopods that existed 65 mya. Using new tools such as DNA analysis, taxonomists continue to look for associations between groups to try to determine which are the ancestral groups and which the more modern.

It is also recognized that if other soft-bodied forms of cephalopods existed earlier than currently thought, there is no fossil evidence available. Perhaps, as more fossils are discovered, new

SCIENTIFIC CLASSIFICATION

The giant Pacific octopus is only one of thousands of different species in the ocean. In order for scientists to ensure that they are all talking about the same animal and not a near relative, the living world has been divided into several parts—four or five kingdoms, depending on which system you choose to use.

A kingdom is the largest of the divisions, and the octopus is in the kingdom Animalae.

The next division is called a phylum, and the octopus is in the phylum Mollusca. This is a huge phylum, which contains many familiar marine and terrestrial animals. Animals such as clams, oysters, scallops, snails, limpets and slugs are all molluscs. They have a common ancestor, and some common features link them together. However, some of the changes that have happened over time make those associations difficult to see.

Within the phylum Mollusca there are further divisions referred to as classes. The octopus is in the class Cephalopoda along with the nautilus, squids, cuttlefishes and a few other odd-looking animals, plus several thousand others that only exist now as fossils. The Latin word "cephalopod" translates as "head-foot." The "head" of a modern octopus or squid contains all the vital organs and organ systems, the brain and a portion of the nerves. The "foot" is modified into a set of appendages called arms and tentacles. The nautilus has a number of arms that all look the same, while octopuses have eight arms but no tentacles. Squids and cuttlefishes have eight arms and two tentacles.

The class Cephalopoda is subdivided into orders. The giant Pacific octopus is in the order Octopoda, which separates the octopuses from the nautiloids, squids and cuttlefishes.

The octopods are subdivided yet again into families, and the giant Pacific octopus is found in the family Octopodidae.

The second smallest division is the genus, and the giant Pacific octopus is in the genus *Enteroctopus*. This now denotes that other octopuses in the genus *Enteroctopus* are very closely related to the giant Pacific octopus.

Lastly, the term species now identifies the giant Pacific octopus on its own. The name used now is *dofleini*.

This naming process is used for every plant and animal as it is described by a scientist. It is based on the common features shared by the rest of the identified plants and animals of the world. This dynamic process constantly undergoes revision as new tools such as DNA analysis change the information we have on a particular group. *Enteroctopus dofleini* is no different than any other animal in that it has been renamed on several occasions.

All scientific names are represented by a genus and species. The name is written with a capital letter for the genus and a lower case letter for the species. In text both names are italicized or underlined but not both. Humans, for example, are *Homo sapiens* or <u>Homo sapiens</u>. The giant Pacific octopus is *Enteroctopus dofleini* or <u>Enteroctopus dofleini</u>.

evidence will lead to a revision of how the cephalopods evolved and what other forms were present in the distant past.

CHARACTERISTICS

Today there are at least 289 species of octopuses in the world, but more are being discovered and described all the time. Some look very different from how we might imagine an octopus to look. For example, a group of deep-water octopuses appears to have ears that they swim with. They have been nicknamed Dumbos after the children's story in which a baby elephant, born with very large ears, was able to fly. The ears are actually fins, but even that is odd, as most octopuses do not have fins.

Most octopuses live on the bottom of the ocean, but some live their entire lives drifting in mid-water. These octopuses are usually transparent and very fragile.

Some species of octopus have developed elaborate colouration or behaviours. The deadly blue-ringed octopus of the South Pacific

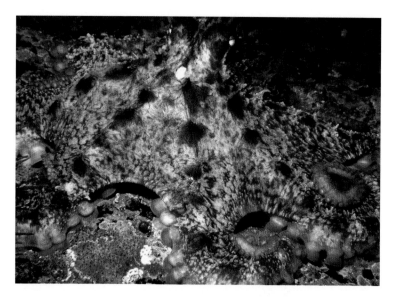

flashes dramatic warnings to potential predators, while others such as the mimic octopus can change shape, colour and behaviour to mimic other more dangerous animals.

Octopuses vary in adult size from small species merely a single gram (0.04 oz) in weight and just a few millimetres long to the giant Pacific octopus, which can reach a weight well over 50 kg (110 lb) and have a radial span—the distance from arm tip to arm tip with the specimen spread out like an umbrella—of more than six metres (20 ft).

All octopuses are marine; they do not live in lakes or rivers. They occur in all the world's oceans and can be found from the polar latitudes to the equator. In addition octopuses are found at all depths and temperatures, although larger species such as the giant Pacific octopus are best adapted to the cold, oxygen-rich water along the coasts of California, Oregon, Washington, BC, Alaska, Russia, northern Japan and Korea. Smaller octopuses tend to live in warmer water that is often closer to the surface or at more tropical latitudes. There are some larger octopuses in tropical waters, but they tend to be found at depths where the water temperature is colder and where there is more dissolved oxygen.

All octopuses are meat eaters (carnivores).

By human standards most octopuses are extremely short-lived. Many grow from a hatched egg to death from old age in less than a single year. The giant Pacific octopus is one of the longer-lived species, going from hatched egg to death from old age in three to three and a half years in BC and perhaps as long as five years in colder waters. As with almost all octopuses, giant Pacific octopuses reproduce only once.

Externally octopuses have a very complex skin containing specialized cells collectively called chromatophores. These are more correctly identified individually as chromatophores (pigment sacs), iridophores (reflective platelets) and leucophores (refractive platelets). These cells are under nervous control and thus enable the octopus to change colour instantly. Octopus skin also contains many small muscles that enable the skin to change

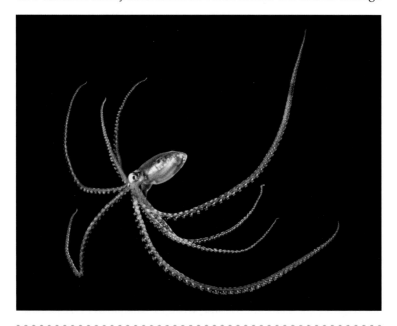

Above: Many species of octopuses and squids are pelagic (open ocean dwellers) for their entire lives. This delicate species was photographed at night at a depth of 20 m (66 ft) in the Coral Sea east of Australia. It is either an undescribed species or the juvenile of a known species. Photo David Fleetham

Opposite: Mottled with brown and red pigments, a giant Pacific octopus blends in with a rocky reef in Barkley Sound on the west coast of Vancouver Island. The white spot below the eyes is a "false eye" intended to confuse a predator. Photo Neil McDaniel

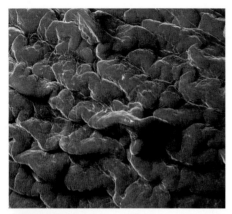

texture from smooth to rough and variations in between. The combination of colour change and skin texture modification enables an octopus to camouflage itself to ambush prey and avoid predators. The giant Pacific octopus, normally tan or brick red, can become dark brown—appearing black in poor light—or white.

The external parts of an octopus that you see are the mantle where all the vital organs—for digestion, excretion, respiration and reproduction—are located along with the gills; the head where the eyes, mouth and brain are located; and the arms (also correctly referred to as legs), which are actually the modified foot of the mollusc.

Opposite top: Complex muscles can rapidly change the texture of the octopus's skin to smooth, ribbed or even spiky with large flattened ridges. Photo Neil McDaniel

Opposite middle: Surrounded by white plumose anemones and yellow sponges, a giant Pacific octopus effectively disguises itself by blanching a mottled white. Photo Neil McDaniel

Opposite bottom: The extraordinary colours and patterns exhibited by the giant Pacific octopus are due to thousands of chromatophores in the skin. Under neuromuscular control, they respond primarily to visual stimuli. This octopus is well camouflaged against a background of small orange tunicates. Photo Neil McDaniel

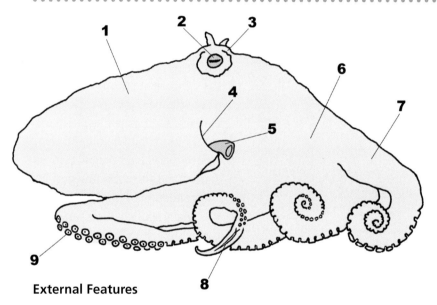

External Features

External features of the octopus are the mantle (1), eye (2), head (3), gill slit (4), siphon or funnel (5), interbrachial web (6), arm or leg (7), hectocotylus (on males only) (8) and suckers (9). Illustration Adrienne Aikins

The mantle is a large muscle that functions like a bellows to draw water in over the gills and then expel it through the siphon. The siphon can be aimed in almost any direction and used to blow ink at a potential predator, push food scraps out of the den, aid in jetting away from a predator or pump water over the eggs when a female is nesting. Strangely, an octopus has three hearts and blue blood (see Chapter Three for more detail on these features).

Continuous from the mantle and head is a tissue that attaches to all the arms to form a web. This interbrachial web aids in catching food and for a movement called jetting.

The head contains a pair of eyes that can focus light to form an image, as can our own eyes, but octopus eyes are also quite different in many ways from those of vertebrates. Also in the head is the mouth, with its bird-like beak, a rasping tongue called a radula and two pairs of salivary glands, one of which contains toxin. Behind the beak is the esophagus, which passes food from the beak to the crop and then the stomach. The esophagus passes through the brain, which forms a ring around the digestive tract. Most of the brain is concerned with the eyes and coordination of body movements such as jetting. Remarkably, more than half of the octopus's nerves are situated in its arms and they can function independently of the brain.

Many publications and TV programs describe octopuses as having tentacles. They do not. Octopuses have only eight arms. Only squids or cuttlefishes have an additional two extensible appendages that are correctly called tentacles. Squids and cuttlefishes are decapods (having 10 appendages); octopuses, as their name suggests, have only eight appendages. To add to the confusion, we also use the word "tentacle" for the approximately 90 appendages of a nautilus, even though these cannot extend as do those of a squid or cuttlefish.

Each arm of an octopus has one or two rows of suckers. On a giant Pacific octopus there are always two rows of suckers, with the smallest suckers located on the tips of the arms and closest to

LIVING FAST, DYING YOUNG

Most octopuses have very short lifespans, many less than one year. The giant Pacific octopus has one of the longest lifespans at approximately four years. Although their lifespan is relatively short, the growth rate of a giant Pacific octopus is amazing. Growing from about 3/100ths of a gram (0.001 oz) to about 20 to 40 kg (44 to 88 lb) is an overall growth rate of about 0.9 percent per day. This makes the octopus one of nature's most efficient carnivores in converting food into increased body mass.

Above: A giant Pacific octopus has two rows of suckers along each arm. They serve many functions including locomotion and the sensing, manipulating and capturing of prey. Photo Neil McDaniel

Right: Taken through the glass of an aquarium, this photograph shows how the suckers flatten out to securely grip surfaces. The delicate outermost skin of the suckers regularly sloughs off. Look for a "ghost" of sloughed skin at the left side of the picture. Photo Brandon Cole

GETTING A GRIP

The adhesive power of octopus suckers is incredible. American zoologist G.H. Parker found that a sucker with a diameter of only 1.3 cm (0.12 in) required a pull of 170 g (six ounces) to break its hold. In theory the grip of the approximately 1,600 suckers of an octopus spanning less than two metres (6.6 ft) would amount to more than 270 kg (595 lb). The largest suckers on a giant Pacific octopus are about 6.4 cm (2.5 in) and can support about 16 kg (35 lb) each. The authors can attest to the fact that when even a small octopus gets a firm grip on smooth rock, a diver stands little chance of dislodging it.

the mouth. The largest suckers are located about one-third of the way along the arm from the mouth.

Octopus suckers are amazing structures. They are far more complex than simple suction cups, since they have both outer and inner chambers. The outer chamber is shaped like a broad suction cup with a reinforced edge and hundreds of fine radial ridges. The ridges are thought to help prevent slipping (shear) when the sucker is attached to a surface that is not perfectly smooth. Small muscles control the shape of the inner chamber, creating the suction force for each individual sucker. Not only can they grasp objects and function independently, but each sucker also functions like a tongue. Octopuses taste what they touch; this ability is called chemotaxis. It enables the octopus to hunt by inserting its arms under rocks and into crevices to find food such as crabs, shrimp and fishes. An octopus does not have to see its prey but can taste it at a distance.

One of our colleagues, Dr. James Wood of the Bermuda Institute of Ocean Sciences, did a simple experiment to see how strong a giant Pacific octopus really might be. He manufactured a small suction-cup device the same size as a large giant Pacific octopus sucker and then used a vacuum to support various weights. When the suction could no longer hold the weight, this was deemed to be the strength of that size of sucker. For a giant Pacific octopus, a large sucker is about 6.4 cm (2.5 in) in diameter.

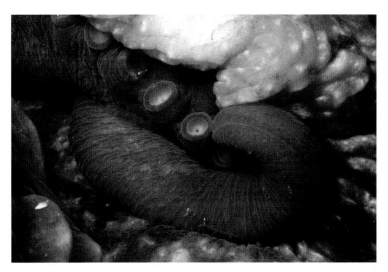

The hectocotylus of a male giant Pacific octopus is the terminal portion of the male's third right arm and has no suckers. The groove functions to grip and transfer the spermatophore during mating. Photo Neil McDaniel

Dr. Wood found that this sucker could support 15.9 kg (35 lb). Given that a mature giant Pacific octopus has approximately 200 suckers per arm and eight arms (1,600 suckers in total), the arithmetic suggests that it would have a total "sucking capacity" of 25,400 kg (56,000 lb). Of course this is an overestimation, because not all the suckers on a giant Pacific octopus are as large as the artificial one used in the test, but even calculating for an average sucker size 50 percent smaller suggests that an octopus could support almost 13 tonnes (14.3 tons). Bottom line: a big giant Pacific octopus is an extremely powerful animal. Divers encountering one should be very careful.

The sex of a giant Pacific octopus can be determined by looking at the third arm on the octopus's right side. If there are suckers all the way to the end of the arm, the octopus is female. If the suckers stop well short of the end of the arm, and there is a groove from there to the tip of the arm, the animal is a male. This modified tip of the male's arm is called a hectocotylus and is used during mating for passing spermatophores (sperm packets) to the female.

DISTRIBUTION

We have only a general idea of where the giant Pacific octopus lives, as with many of the world's octopuses. Current research shows that giant Pacific octopuses range along the Pacific coast of North America from southern California northward along the coasts of Oregon, Washington, BC and Alaska, and then west and south along the coasts of Russia and northern Japan, all the way to Korea.

Giant Pacific octopuses live from the intertidal zone down to depths of 2,000 m (6,600 ft). It might seem odd that giant Pacific octopuses inhabit the intertidal zone, but in Alaska, where there are many sea otters that hunt them, the octopuses have established themselves in dens under large rocks that are exposed at low tide. They actually live above the tide line for a while each day and come out to hunt when the water rises and covers the eelgrass beds. On the BC coast, sea otters were exterminated dur-

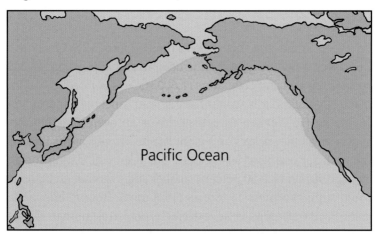

Pacific Ocean

Above: Giant Pacific octopuses range throughout the North Pacific from Korea, east across the Aleutian Islands and south along the Pacific coast of North America to southern California.
Illustration Adrienne Aikins

Opposite: Jim (red drysuit) and assistant David Pickles complete the weighing, sexing and tagging (note yellow disc on the arm) of a young octopus. Data collected from recaptures of tagged animals were used to establish growth rates and patterns.
Photo Fred Bavendam

ing the fur trade, so in most areas giant Pacific octopuses can live in shallow water without risk of predation by sea otters. Since Alaskan sea otters were transplanted to the west coast of Vancouver Island in the 1970s, their population has grown and expanded in range. It remains to be seen how the reintroduction of sea otters  will affect the distribution of giant Pacific octopuses.

Where individual giant octopuses choose to live is still a bit of a mystery. About 20 years ago Jim had the fortunate opportunity to work with highly respected cephalopod researcher Dr. Jennifer Mather on a project in Saanich Inlet, north of Victoria. The researchers attached electronic tags to individual octopuses, and the location of each one was tracked every 15 minutes for as long as the battery in the tag lasted or until the four-week project ended. The results showed that each octopus had an extensive home range of about 250 m (800 ft) by 250 m, or about the size of eight city blocks. Each octopus overlapped the home ranges of other octopuses from 37 percent to as much as 99 percent, so their ranges were clearly not territories with well-defined or defended boundaries. Octopuses moved in and out of the study site on an irregular basis. This project also discovered that giant Pacific octopuses make longer hunting trips during the night and shorter trips in daylight. The trips are often from one den to another so that food caught along the way can be eaten in safety.

Japanese researchers using a tag-and-recapture method of study found that one octopus travelled more than two kilometres (1.2 mi) in less than 24 hours. The Japanese also discovered that giant Pacific octopuses migrate twice a year from shallow water to deep water and back. Fluctuations in water temperature change the water currents, and octopuses follow the cooler water. In the northeast Pacific, on the other hand, no one has demonstrated mass migrations of giant Pacific octopuses. In fact the

Above: In some early scientific work, Jim tried a number of different methods of tagging giant Pacific octopuses. This method made the tag easy to see even while the animal was in the den, but it was eventually abandoned, as some octopuses damaged their mantles by pulling off the tag.
Photo Jim Cosgrove

Right: Jim holds a small specimen that has just been captured as part of a growth-rate study. Jim weighed, sexed and tagged the octopus in less than three minutes and returned it to its den. Photo Fred Bavendam

octopuses stay on the North American coast all year round instead of migrating.

A five-year study by Jim, also using a tag-and-recapture method, showed that 50 percent of the octopuses moved out of the research area immediately after their initial capture, and researchers never found them again. Several of those recaptured had more than one den, and one animal was recaptured seven times over 202 days.

These and other studies suggest that giant Pacific octopuses do not establish a permanent home but change dens as they grow larger. They move for any number of reasons, including a decrease in local food availability, a change in water quality, an increase in predation or an increased population of octopuses resulting in too few suitable dens.

Biology

How do octopuses breathe, capture food, sense their surroundings and avoid predators? And how big do they really get? This chapter presents the inside story of how octopuses survive and thrive in the marine environment.

TRIPLE HEARTS AND BLUE BLOOD

Octopuses have not one, not two, but three hearts! These are not multi-chambered hearts like ours; they're simpler, yet they serve the same purpose. Octopuses have two or four gills called ctenidia. The giant Pacific octopus has just two gills, one on each side, just inside the opening to the mantle.

When an octopus inhales sea water, the longitudinal muscles of its mantle contract to suck water into the mantle. Water passes over the gills, where oxygen is exchanged with carbon dioxide just as in our lungs. The blood, now enriched with oxygen, is pumped by hearts at the base of the gills (branchial hearts) to the main heart (the somatic heart). The somatic heart then pumps the blood throughout the body, where oxygen is exchanged for carbon dioxide. Nutrients are absorbed and moved to cells, while wastes are transported to the kidneys. The oxygen-depleted blood circulates back to the branchial hearts, and the cycle repeats. The water

that was breathed in is expelled when the circular muscles of the mantle contract, forcing the water out through the funnel.

The blood itself is very different from that of a vertebrate such as a human. Octopuses are truly among the invertebrate nobility, as they actually have blue blood. Our blood is bright red when saturated with oxygen and dark red when oxygen poor. The reddish colour of our blood is due to the iron base in our blood pigment called hemoglobin.

● ●

Above: The breathing cycle: This giant Pacific octopus has just expanded its bag-like mantle to draw water in over the gills through gill slits on either side. Next the valves in the mantle openings close, and the water is forced out through the funnel.
Photo Neil McDaniel

Opposite: **The Respiratory System**

Water is drawn into the mantle through the pair of gill slits (1) where it passes over the gills (2). Blood in the gills releases carbon dioxide and picks up oxygen and transports it from the gills to one of the two branchial hearts (3). Then the blood is pumped to the somatic or visceral heart (4), where it is sent to the rest of the body. The oxygen-depleted water is exhausted from the mantle via the funnel or siphon (5). Illustration Adrienne Aikins

● ●

In octopuses the blood pigment is a copper-based compound called hemocyanin. It has a pale blue colour when it is oxygenated and is nearly clear when oxygen-depleted. Unfortunately for octopuses, they cannot endure a long struggle, largely because hemocyanin is not a very efficient oxygen carrier. They run out of energy in a matter of minutes.

In addition to the challenges posed by the inefficient hemocyanin, oxygen is present in water at far lower levels than in air. Air consists of almost 21 percent oxygen, while the oxygen dissolved in sea water is but a tiny fraction of 1 percent (about nine parts per million at 10°C or 50°F in 3.4 percent sea water). Humans can do effective rescue breathing—mouth-to-mouth resuscitation—because we only use a small portion of the oxygen in each breath

THREE HEARTS BEATING AS ONE

Octopuses have three hearts. One heart is located at the base of each of the gills and is called a branchial heart. The two branchial hearts take oxygen-depleted blood returning from the body and pump it through the gills, where carbon dioxide is given off and oxygen is absorbed. The third and largest heart, called the somatic heart, pumps oxygenated blood from the gills to the rest of the body. Octopus blood is pale blue when it is oxygenated and almost clear when it is oxygen-depleted. Octopuses are truly the "blue bloods" of the ocean.

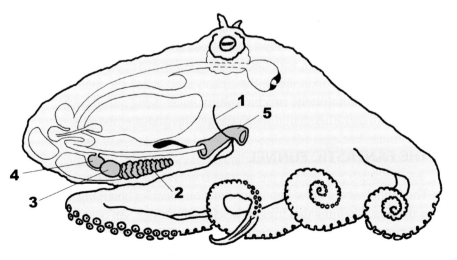

contractions of the mantle, and the funnel directs the jet of water downward below the arms, which fan out into a crude wing shape. This concentrated blast of water pushes the octopus through the water mantle first, and the lift provided by the wing-shaped body enables the octopus to "fly" considerable distances. A jetting giant Pacific octopus usually cannot out-swim a diver for long, but if it gets a bit of a head start, it may well escape into deeper water.

DISMAL DIGESTION

One anatomical feature of the octopus that sets it apart from squid is its digestive system. The first structure for food gathering is the interbrachial web, the umbrella-like membrane between the arms that the octopus uses to enfold food such as crabs, shrimps and sometimes even fishes or birds. The web forms a bag-like container that holds prey close to the mouth. Squids and cuttlefishes use their extensible, sucker-covered tentacles for the initial capture of food.

The second structure is the mouth. An octopus has two pair of salivary glands, anterior (front) and posterior (rear). The posterior salivary glands produce a toxin called a cephalotoxin. In giant Pacific octopuses this is not known to be deadly to humans, whereas in the blue-ringed octopuses of the South Pacific it has killed people. When an octopus captures food in its web, it

Resembling a parrot's beak, the giant Pacific octopus's chitinous beak is the hardest part of its body. The tips of this beak are well-worn from crunching hard-shelled prey and have lost their sharp cutting edges.
Photo Jim Cosgrove

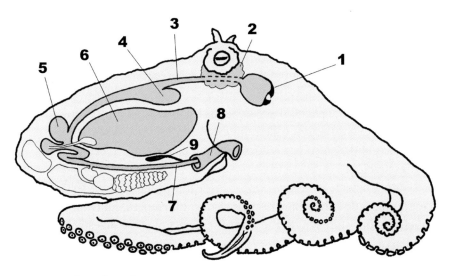

The Digestive System

Food is captured by the suckers and held up to the beak (1), where it is chopped into small pieces. Inside a tube, the food passes through the brain (2) and along the esophagus (3) to the crop (4), where it can be stored for a short period of time. The food then progresses to the blind stomach (5), where enzymes are added from the liver (6). Waste products are moved from the stomach via the intestine (7) and are expelled through the siphon (8). The ink sac (9) also empties into the siphon.

Illustration Adrienne Aikins

secretes cephalotoxin into the water, where it is absorbed through the gills of the prey. This neurotoxin affects the nervous system and causes the prey to lose consciousness and stop struggling. The octopus can then use its suckers to aid in dismembering prey such as a crab.

The beak, the hardest part of an octopus, is made of the same chitinous material as human fingernails. It is black and looks like the beak of a parrot. The mouth also has a specialized tongue called a radula. This file-like organ is covered with tiny, sharp teeth that are replaced when they wear down, much as sharks regrow teeth. The radular teeth shred the prey's tissue once the beak has bitten the food into small chunks. Working together with the beak and radula are secretions of the anterior (front) salivary gland. This gland produces a mixture of substances called enzymes, which cause the food to break down quickly into a jelly-like substance that can be easily digested. A combination of the enzymes and the radula enables an octopus to winkle even the tiniest bit of tissue out of the tip of a crab's leg.

Once the food is captured, eaten and swallowed, it travels along a short tube called the esophagus (similar to the throat in a human) to a structure called the crop. This is not exactly the same as a bird's crop, but it does function as a storage place for undigested food.

If the stomach is empty, food passes immediately from the crop to the stomach, which despite distinct differences, functions much like our stomach. In the giant Pacific octopus the digestive

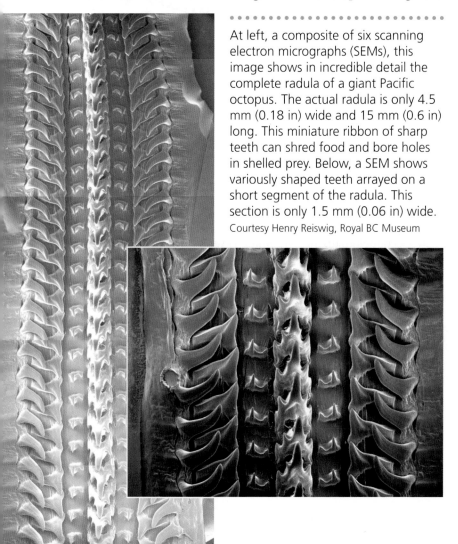

At left, a composite of six scanning electron micrographs (SEMs), this image shows in incredible detail the complete radula of a giant Pacific octopus. The actual radula is only 4.5 mm (0.18 in) wide and 15 mm (0.6 in) long. This miniature ribbon of sharp teeth can shred food and bore holes in shelled prey. Below, a SEM shows variously shaped teeth arrayed on a short segment of the radula. This section is only 1.5 mm (0.06 in) wide.
Courtesy Henry Reiswig, Royal BC Museum

enzymes do not come from the wall of the stomach but are produced by the liver and introduced into the stomach through ducts. These enzymes cause the food to break down into small molecules that the blood absorbs and transports back to the liver. There they are processed and distributed into the cells of the body. This dual-function liver is different from a human's, whose liver primarily deals with the products of digested food.

Now we find another major difference from vertebrates such as humans and also from squids. Once the food in the octopus stomach is digested, the waste material has to be evacuated. The octopus stomach, however,

THE GUTS OF THE ISSUE

The stomach of the octopus has only one tube that takes food into the stomach and then removes the waste. This limits the amount of energy an octopus can gain in a short period of time. Once processed, the waste food is pushed out of the stomach into the intestine, where it is shunted into the funnel and blown out into the water.

has only a single tube leading in and out. This means that the waste material must be evacuated through the same tube the food entered before more food can be introduced for digestion. You might call this "digestion on the installment plan." The waste comes out of the stomach into the intestine, which encapsulates it and moves it along until it eventually reaches the end of the intestine located at the entrance to the funnel. Octopus poop, ejected from the funnel, looks a bit like a slender red ribbon.

The differences in liver function and the blind gut distinguish octopuses from squids. In squids the liver functions much as in vertebrates, as an absorptive organ. Squids also have a stomach with separate entrance and exit tubes, so food can be continuously introduced and processed and waste can be removed without delay.

In giant Pacific octopuses the processing of food, depending on what is being eaten, can take many hours. On average these octopuses make six hunting trips a day, reposing in their den most of the time while they process food.

THE HOUDINI OF THE SEA

The giant Pacific octopus has no bones. Other than its beak it has no hard parts at all, and this enables it to crawl through unbelievably small openings. An octopus quickly learns that crab traps are a potential source of quick and easy meals. Since the crabs cannot get out of the trap, an octopus only has to figure out how to get at them. It might try to catch a crab with one or two arms and pull it out of the trap and under its web. Once it discovers that this won't work (and probably results in a nasty pinch), it might crawl through the wire mesh into the trap and subdue one or more crabs with its toxin, trapping them under its web. An experienced giant Pacific octopus knows that it cannot leave the trap with the crabs and starts to take them apart and store the food in its crop. Once it eats the crabs, it discards the shells and squeezes its way out of the trap, then wanders back to its den, where it waits to process the food and become hungry again.

This lack of bones also makes an octopus an incredible escape artist. There are many stories of divers and aquarists who have captured an octopus and put it into a tank or aquarium where they felt it was perfectly well contained, only to return and find that it had escaped.

At one point in Jim's career, he worked as a lab assistant at a junior college. One of his tasks was to collect specimens for an invertebrate zoology course. For Mollusc Week he had collected local molluscs including chitons, limpets, jingle oysters, scallops, clams, swimming scallops, mussels, an assortment of nudibranchs, snails and a small giant Pacific octopus. Knowing that the octopus would likely eat much of the collection before the labs finished, he put it into a separate aquarium. Well aware of octopod escape-artist skills, he put a heavy lid on the aquarium.

When he came in to work the next day, he discovered that the giant Pacific octopus had somehow managed to push the lid off. It had squirted most of the water out of the aquarium and onto the floor of the lab, creating a small stream that ran from the aquarium toward the drain. It had vacated its tank and crawled down the water path, continuing for some distance until it eventually hit a wall—literally—and unfortunately died.

Jim's second experience had a happier ending but was a much greater mystery. He recalled, "As part of my collecting duties for a University of Victoria comparative physiology class, I had collected a small octopus and put it into an aquarium called an Instant Ocean™. An Instant Ocean™ looks like a typical 225 l (50 gal) aquarium with a below-gravel filter and two surface skimmers, which empty into a 365 l (80 gal) storage reservoir hidden below the display aquarium. In the reservoir the water is chilled and pumped back up to the display aquarium.

"The instructor of the class was aware of what I had brought in for the lab, so I was surprised to get a phone call asking where the octopus was. I told her it was in the aquarium, but she said that it wasn't. Sure enough, it was gone. Over the next four or five weeks, we continued to have specimens go missing, and I was sure that someone was stocking their home aquarium at our expense. It was both annoying for me and awkward for the instructor, who had to manage without much-needed specimens.

"By now it was late February and getting dark outside by 4:30 p.m. I had stayed late at the university to work on a project, and it was about 10:00 p.m. before I headed for home. As I walked by the physiology lab, I popped in just to be sure that what I had recently collected was still there. Imagine my surprise when I flipped on the room lights and was confronted by the sight of the octopus placidly sitting in the tank! Imagine my further surprise as the octopus pushed the aquarium cover up, crawled over to one of the surface skimmers and proceeded to slither down the pipe into the storage reservoir below the display aquarium. The next day the mystery was resolved as we drained and removed the display aquarium to reveal a very contented (and considerably plumper) giant Pacific octopus with the remains of some of the missing specimens in the reservoir. That sneaky giant Pacific octopus was released in the ocean and I made a point of never putting an octopus into an Instant Ocean™ again."

SEEING YOU

Given that an octopus has no bones, it obviously has no skull. This results in its interesting way of seeing. An octopus's eyesight is excellent, and has been compared to that of most vertebrates. It sees in black and white, the same as a dog or cat.

In vertebrates the skull holds the eyeballs in fixed positions, so we can only look forward and a short distance sideways without turning our heads. Having both eyes view the same scene but from slightly different positions gives us the ability to judge distance and to be very accurate when reaching out to pick up objects. Human eyes deal with incoming light by using our eye muscles to thicken or thin the lens to focus light on a fixed point,

Experiments have shown that giant Pacific octopuses have excellent eyesight, as keen as the vision of fishes and many other vertebrates. The retina contains only one visual pigment, so they are considered to be colour-blind. Photo Neil McDaniel

our retina. When our eyes cannot focus the light exactly, our blurred vision requires corrective eyewear. Also, we cannot see underwater without first having light pass through the air pocket in our face masks.

An octopus has no skull holding the eyes fixed in place, though, so it can do several things vertebrates cannot. The octopus can move its eyes independently so one can be watching in

THE EYES HAVE IT

The octopus has excellent eyesight but is colour-blind, which is surprising in an animal that relies on colour to camouflage itself. So how can octopuses do such an amazing job of hiding? Experimentation has shown that octopuses try to match the reflected light levels of their surroundings as well as resembling the texture of their surroundings.

one direction while the other is looking in the other. Birds such as pigeons have eyes on the sides of their heads and have restricted vision directly in front of and behind them. An octopus, however, can move its eyes forward and see over a wide field of view. The eye of the octopus has a fixed lens, and its muscles attach to the eyeball itself. To focus light on the retina, the octopus adjusts the shape of the eyeball. This is the opposite of the vertebrate eye's process but achieves the same result.

The prime function of the chromatophores is to enable an octopus or squid to camouflage and avoid predation. In squids and cuttlefishes the chromatophores also aid in communication, especially during mating. That may also be true in octopuses, but is unproven for giant Pacific octopuses.

Predators seek out any feature that makes it easier for them to locate and capture prey. It has been this way for millions of years, and there are many examples of plants and animals adapting to changes in their environment. An often-asked question is how an octopus, which sees only in black and white, knows what colour or pattern of colours to camouflage itself to avoid predators. An octopus that failed to assume the correct colour or displayed inappropriate behaviour in response to a predator would likely be captured and no longer contribute to the gene pool. Over the history of our planet many species have become extinct, and some of those extinctions are due to the inability of organisms to adapt quickly enough to changing conditions.

An octopus doesn't make a conscious decision on what colour to turn when confronted by a sea lion; this is an innate (built-in) response that has evolved over millions of years. If you transferred a giant Pacific octopus to another ocean, where it had to deal with predators that it has never been exposed to before, there is a high probability that it would either be very successful or that it would be wiped out. Look at what happens when foreign plants and animals (called invasive species) are introduced into new habitats. It is estimated that the islands of Hawaii have lost more than 90 percent of their indigenous flora and fauna, which could not compete with the introduced invasive species. On the flip side, the introduced flora and fauna are often successful because none of their normal predators are present to keep them in check.

WHAT'S EATING YOU?

Giant Pacific octopuses, like almost all plants and animals, are hosts to a variety of parasites, both endoparasites that live inside the animal and ectoparasites that live on the outside. For example, an entire group of multicellular animals called dicyemids live only in cephalopod kidneys. Other cephalopod endoparasites include protozoans, nematodes and flatworms. Ectoparasites tend to be less numerous; parasitic copepods are the most common and the easiest for a diver to see. An octopus's health can suffer when the animal is infested with large numbers of these sea lice. Small marine leeches have also been found on cephalopods, including giant Pacific octopuses.

HOW BIG IS BIG?

What is the world's largest octopus and how big does it get? These are much-discussed questions. There are many anecdotal reports from divers and fishers of really huge giant Pacific octopuses, but all describe their encounters in different ways. Some describe the octopus as filling a rocky den, goody bag, crab trap,

Giant Pacific octopuses sometimes bear external parasites. Several marine leeches cling to the funnel of this animal. Frame from video, Neil McDaniel

bottom of a boat or bucket. That's all well and good, but unless we know the volume of the container, it's impossible to even hazard an estimate of the octopus's weight and radial span.

While carrying out an octopus tagging project, Jim also surveyed the divers working on the research team. The project involved three or four weekly dives to locate and capture octopuses. Each animal was removed from the water and quickly sexed, weighed and tagged. If it already had a tag, researchers recorded the number and reweighed the octopus. Then a diver took it back into the water and returned it to the vicinity of its den. Before the octopus was weighed, Jim asked each diver on the team to estimate how much it weighed. At first their errors were very large, but with experience the divers estimated within a kilogram (2.2 lb) for octopuses up to 15 kg (33 lb) and more accurately for smaller animals. For animals over 20 kg (44 lb) they were less accurate, and the error rate increased, but this varied from diver to diver with some consistently more accurate than others. These experienced divers were dealing regularly with captured octopuses, yet even they had difficulty in estimating the weight of large animals. The probability is that inexperienced divers and non-divers who have never weighed an octopus would quite likely overestimate the size of a captured animal.

So back to the burning questions. How big is the biggest octopus in the world? And is the giant Pacific octopus the largest species?

The second question seems easiest to answer. Yes, the giant Pacific octopus is by far the largest species in the world . . . unless there is another species of octopus that is currently undocumented by a specimen. In 1896 the rotted remains of some sort of massive animal were found on the beach in St. Augustine, Florida. It was originally identified as a new species of octopus, *Octopus giganteus*, but—despite contrary opinions—modern DNA analysis has revealed it to be tissue from a sperm whale.

Many years ago some scientists speculated about the existence of an octopus species that was very large but exceedingly rare. It lived in the same range as the giant Pacific octopus, some people believed, but the juveniles were misidentified as large giant Pacific octopuses. The real giants were thought to live far too deep for divers to observe and were so huge that they evaded all common methods of fishing.

There are indeed other very hefty species of octopuses that have been captured. In New Zealand an octopus called *Haliphron atlanticus* was hauled up from 900 m (3,000 ft) in a fishing net. The damaged specimen, reportedly four metres (13 ft) in total length—from the tip of the mantle to the end of the longest arm—and weighing 75 kg (165 lb), is currently retained for further study by the New Zealand National Institute of Water and Atmospheric Research (NIWA).

Guinness World Records, which is highly respected for its research to confirm its records, lists the world's largest octopus as weighing 136 kg (300 lb) and having an arm span of 9.8 m (32 ft), and confirms that the giant Pacific octopus is the world's largest species.

Dr. Murray Newman, former director of the Vancouver Aquarium, tells in his 1994 book *Life in a Fishbowl* of a 198 kg (437 lb) octopus that was captured by Jock MacLean near Port Hardy, BC, in March 1956. It was reported to have a radial span of 8.5 m (28 ft) and completely filled a 205 l (45 gal) barrel.

A second enormous specimen was collected by Jock MacLean in 1957, again in the Port Hardy area. Jock estimated that it weighed an incredible 272 kg (600 lb) and had a radial span of 9.8 m (32 ft). As this specimen was not actually put on a scale or measured with a tape, the accuracy of these values is questionable. As Jim's studies have shown, even experienced divers consistently overestimate the weight of big animals.

In 1873 and again in 1885, Professor William H. Dall of the United States National Museum (now the Smithsonian Institution) reported on two huge octopuses captured in Alaska. The first, taken near Sitka, was described as having a radial span of 8.5 m (28 ft) and a total length of 4.9 m (16 ft). The second animal was speared at Iliuliuk, Unalaska Island, and described as having a radial span of 9.8 m (32 ft) and a total length of 4.9 m (16 ft). No weights were reported for either animal and they were not retained for further study. But the adventurous Dall did try cooking some of his catch. He noted, "Having heard octopus were eatable, and the flesh looking white and clean, we boiled some sections of the arms in salt and water, but found them so tough and elastic that our teeth could not make the slightest impression upon them."

In 1945 a huge octopus was captured off Santa Barbara, California, that was reported to weigh 182 kg (402 lb). Fortunately a photograph of this beast was taken, and it is clearly a very large animal. The way the octopus is displayed makes it difficult to estimate size, but if the man in the photo is of average height, this octopus would have been over three metres (10 ft) long, depending on how much of the arms is lying on the ground; it likely had a radial span of 6 to 6.7 m (20 to 22 ft). Although this photo raises some questions, it is still one of the better pieces of evidence we have regarding the maximum size of this species, presuming this is in fact a giant Pacific octopus.

Another old photograph in the collections of the Seattle Aquarium shows a large octopus captured off Vashon Island in Washington state in the 1940s. This animal was reported to weigh 95 kg (210 lb).

Above: A badly faded photograph from the 1940s shows a 95.3 kg (210 lb) giant Pacific octopus captured at Vashon Island, Washington. This is the largest giant Pacific octopus currently on record from that state. Courtesy Seattle Aquarium

Opposite: Fisher Babe Castagnola poses beside a huge octopus that was caught in 1945 after it came to the surface clinging to a lobster trap off Santa Cruz Island, California. The animal weighed 182.3 kg (402 lb), but its radial span was not measured. The photograph suggests a radial span of about six metres (20 ft). Courtesy Castagnola Restaurant

Twin brothers Frank and John McGuire became commercial divers in 1960 and formed a company called Underwater Unlimited to supply marine creatures to aquariums from California to BC. They hunted octopuses in the waters near Victoria for many years and caught several monsters in excess of 45 kg (100 lb). The largest octopus that Jim has ever seen was a 71 kg (156 lb) beast captured by the McGuires while they were employees of the Undersea Gardens when it was located where the Oak Bay Marina is now sited. The eight-armed giant was collected off a marker on Johnstone Reef near Ten Mile Point in the mid-1960s (see Chapter Seven for Jim's memorable encounter).

Above: One of the largest giant Pacific octopuses ever on public display, this monster was captured by Frank and John McGuire of Victoria and exhibited at the Undersea Gardens in Oak Bay. This beast gave Jim a thorough thrashing during one of his shows (see Chapter Seven). Courtesy McGuire Family

Opposite: The red rock crab (*Cancer productus*) is the favourite prey of many giant Pacific octopuses. Even though it is agile and has strong claws, this crustacean is no match for its eight-armed adversaries. Photo Neil McDaniel

Dr. Roland Anderson of the Seattle Aquarium has long been on the lookout for a giant Pacific octopus in excess of 45 kg (100 lb) but has never found one. As an experiment Anderson tried to raise a monster octopus by feeding a large male all the food it would accept. When it finally died it was 43 kg (95 lb), and its largest suckers were 7.9 cm (3.1 in) in diameter.

Anderson has also studied the concentration of heavy metals and PCBs in the tissues of giant Pacific octopuses from Puget Sound. He found high concentrations in their digestive glands, likely obtained from their primary prey, red rock crabs (*Cancer productus*). These crabs bury themselves in contaminated sediments and eat prey that live in polluted substrates. He suggests that man-made pollution may cause giant Pacific octopuses to mature at smaller sizes and thus be a reason why very large octopuses are rarely seen these days.

All the really big octopuses seem to have been captured more than 50 years ago. This has been confirmed by interviews with active commercial octopus harvesters who have captured thousands of giant Pacific octopuses over the past 20 years. None of them has captured a giant Pacific octopus weighing in excess of 57 kg (125 lb).

A rare 1912 photograph shows a cheerful group in Avalon, California, displaying a large giant Pacific octopus that was caught off Santa Catalina Island. Its size and weight were not recorded. Courtesy Catalina Island Museum

How big is the largest octopus in the world? The specimen William Dall speared in 1885 at Iliuliuk had the largest radial span of any giant Pacific octopus ever measured. Jock MacLean's 1956 Port Hardy behemoth was the biggest ever weighed. The Santa Barbara specimen photographed in 1945 was the second heaviest. It would appear that octopuses weighing as much as 272 kg (600 lb) and with radial spans of over nine metres (30 ft) are within the realm of possibility, but have never actually been documented by both measuring and weighing.

Is there another unknown and undescribed species of octopus that is even bigger than the giant Pacific octopus? If there is such an animal, where has it gone and why have we not seen one in the past 50 years? We don't think there is another species. What we are seeing, we believe, is a species adapting to changing ocean conditions by gradually getting smaller in size. We doubt that we will see many 45 kg (100 lb) giant Pacific octopuses in the future. The evidence to disprove this theory would be a very large captured octopus that could be examined with proper scientific rigour to establish whether or not we have a new, undescribed species or just a rare, really big giant Pacific octopus. The ocean is vast, and there is so much that we still don't understand. Who knows what might lurk in the depths!

There has long been a difference of scientific opinion on whether there is only one species of giant Pacific octopus or whether several subspecies inhabit different parts of the North Pacific. Sorting out that particular puzzle would be a major scientific undertaking. A researcher would have to obtain specimens from Japan, Korea, Russia, Alaska, BC, Washington, Oregon and California and compare all the physical and biochemical details of those specimens. The data could then be analyzed to determine if there is a statistical argument about whether or not there are enough differences to assign subspecies or even split the species and describe new species.

Details of the behaviours of the specimens also need to be accounted for. It is just as legitimate to assign new species on the basis of unique behaviours as it is to use anatomical or biochemical features. For example, if the giant Pacific octopuses in Japan only mated in water cooler than 8°C (46°F) and the giant Pacific octopuses from California never mated in water cooler than 10°C (50°F), it might indicate a difference between the two populations. Another approach would be to take giant Pacific octopus eggs from Japan and raise the paralarvae in BC waters to see what weight they finally achieved. Anyone looking for a fascinating PhD study?

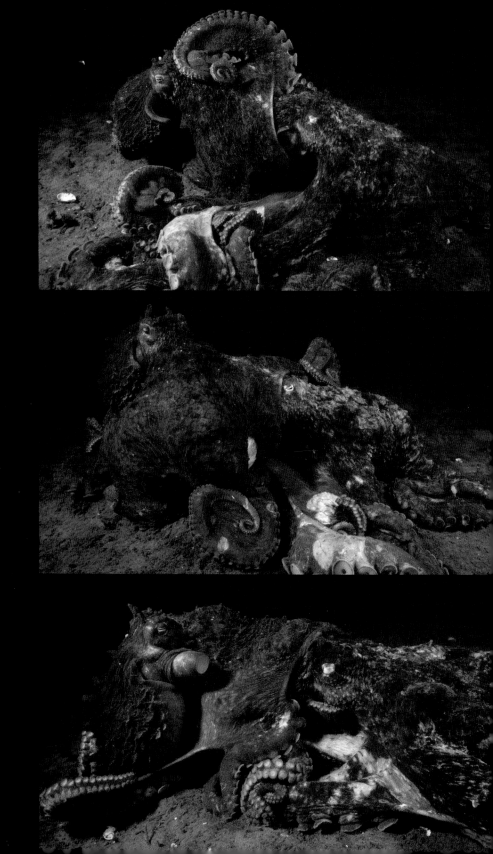

Reproduction

Jim's research for more than 15 years focussed on the reproductive aspects of the giant Pacific octopus's life history. This was not well understood, a serious shortcoming when a commercial harvest is taking place.

Most cephalopods reproduce only once; this was thought to be true of the giant Pacific octopus as well. For many cephalopods, when a female mates and lays her eggs, she tends them for a period of time and then dies. If this was true for giant Pacific octopuses, then any octopus harvested was prereproductive. Almost nothing was understood of the male's life after mating. Obviously no species can be harvested for any length of time if the adults never have the opportunity to replace themselves.

Both sexes mature at the same rate and appear to reach sexual maturity at about 32 months in southern BC waters. At this time both the males and females weigh about 15 to 18 kg (33 to 40 lb).

Mating giant Pacific octopuses are rarely observed, let alone photographed. In this remarkable sequence of images, the male (on the left) partially envelops a somewhat larger female. Not visible in this tangle of arms is the male's third right arm tip, which he uses to insert his sperm packet into the female's mantle cavity.
Photos Fred Bavendam

In Jim's research areas near Victoria, he noted two peaks in the maturation of the giant octopus population. The first and larger peak was in November and December, the second and smaller peak in April.

FINDING A MATE...OR NINE?

When a female giant Pacific octopus is ready to mate, it appears that she selects a den and attracts males to her. There is no conclusive evidence on how the female entices males, but there are strong indications that she produces some sort of chemical attractant. There are several reasons for believing this to be true.

The first reason is that giant Pacific octopuses are ordinarily solitary, and a smaller female would normally avoid a larger male that might attack and eat her. Jim has seen as many as nine males, however, in the immediate proximity of a female in a den. The males were scattered around the den and appeared to be unaware of each other, as there were no interactions amongst them. This was most unusual.

The second reason is that Jim has observed and seen video of large males standing atop prominent rocks. The octopus faces into the current and spreads out his arms like an open umbrella, turning slowly back and forth as the current flows past. We know that octopus suckers are sensitive chemical sensors, so it's likely that the male tastes the water flowing past. His slow turning may enable him to identify the direction of the female's attractant.

How the female selects a male—and whether she mates with one or more than one male—are still unknown. Jim is currently working with a genetics professor at the University of Victoria to try to resolve these questions.

Once a female selects a male, there are several ways in which the male transfers sperm to her. Sometimes the male mounts the female, almost completely covering her. In other cases the male merely extends his hectocotylized third right arm into the female's den. Although the actual transfer of sperm requires only two to four hours, the mating process can last several days, so divers have a considerable handicap when trying to observe such behaviour. Indeed it is a rare event to witness a mating pair, and

Jim has only seen nine matings. This is one situation in which observations in an aquarium are far easier than those in the open ocean. An aquarium researcher can set up a video camera and organize teams to watch the process on a 24-hour schedule until the event ends.

Jim, along with three other researchers, has combined experiences from open ocean and aquarium observations to produce a publication about giant Pacific octopus matings. The study revealed that the male and female mate for approximately four hours and that repeat matings have been observed. In aquariums there is usually only one male in the tank with the female, so questions about multiple males and how the female selects a particular mate remain unanswered.

HIGH SPERM COUNT

The male giant Pacific octopus passes sperm to the female in an elongate package called a spermatophore. The spermatophore can be up to one metre (3 ft) long and contain over four billion sperm cells.

The male passes the female an elongated package of sperm called a spermatophore, which may be up to one metre (three feet) long, which he deposits in one of the female's two oviducts. It is believed that when mating the male actually places two spermatophores in the female, one at the entrance to each oviduct. At this time the female is not yet pregnant—the term really does not apply to invertebrates anyway—but she has stored the sperm and will head off to find a suitable den to lay her eggs. The male, if he still has unused spermatophores, may try to find another female.

The den the female selects is usually deeper than 20 m (66 ft). Jim has noted that dens where previous females have nested were reused 41 percent of the time. These preferred dens tend to be under large flat rocks that provide a suitable overhead surface for the female to attach her eggs.

Once the female selects the den, she sometimes fortifies it by gathering rocks from the surrounding area and dragging them to the den. She often piles them up to create a wall of boulders that keeps out predators. A few days to a month may elapse between mating and selecting and preparing a den.

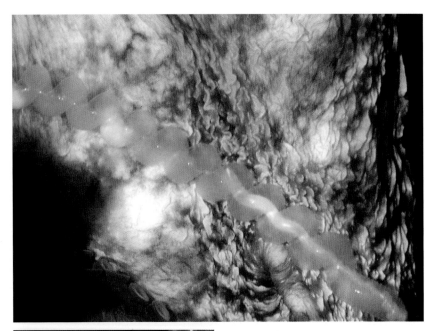

Above: A male giant Pacific octopus produces spermatophores, which contain the sperm that he will deposit inside the female's mantle. Contained within the outer curled tube of this spermatophore is another tube containing up to four billion sperm.
Photo Sandra Palm, Seattle Aquarium

Left: The spermatophore can be up to one metre (3 ft) in length. The pale area at the tip of the spermatophore is where the outer tube ruptures, allowing the sperm to flow into the female's oviduct.
Photo Sandra Palm, Seattle Aquarium

LAYING THE EGGS

Now the female begins to lay her eggs. She turns upside down and clings to the roof of the den while she lays the tiny eggs one at a time. Each egg is produced in the ovary and coated with rich yolk to provide energy for the developing embryo. At this point some sperm is used to fertilize the egg, and it is coated with a material that hardens into a rubbery, semi-opaque shell. Each egg is extruded individually through the funnel and grasped by the small suckers that surround the mother's mouth.

The body of the egg is a mere six millimetres (0.2 in) long—about the size of a grain of rice—with a slender tail that adds another 11 mm (0.4 in), making the total length of the egg about 17 mm (0.7 in). The mother's small suckers deftly manipulate the tail of the egg along with the tails of other eggs and weave them together into a slender string. She produces a secretion and applies it to the tails to bind them together. Over a period of three or four hours, while hanging upside down, the female produces a string containing an average of 176 eggs. Having glued this string to the roof of the den, the female descends to rest before returning to lay another string.

Eventually, over 28 to 42 days, the female will produce a complete nest of about 390 strings with approximately 68,000 eggs.

NESTING BEHAVIOUR: THE LONG WAIT

Once the female has finished laying, she spends the next 6.5 to 11 months tending the eggs. She grooms them with her suckers to keep them free of bacteria and other organisms that might damage them. Usually she is not completely successful, as often some eggs are encrusted by colonial animals called hydroids and do not hatch.

The female blows water through the strings of eggs with enough force that they jostle around. This helps keep them clean and free of growth and will be critical when the eggs start to hatch. She also protects the nest against predators such as sea stars, not always successfully. Mottled sea stars (*Evasterias troschelii*) have been observed robbing egg strings from a den.

Top: Before she lays her eggs, a female selects a den and often builds a wall of rocks to keep predators out. This well-crafted wall will remain intact until the female knocks it down in seven to 10 months' time just before she dies. Photo Jim Cosgrove

Bottom: The white colour of the eggs indicates that this is a fairly new nest. The female grooms the eggs with gentle movements of her arms and streams of water blown through her funnel. Photo Jim Cosgrove

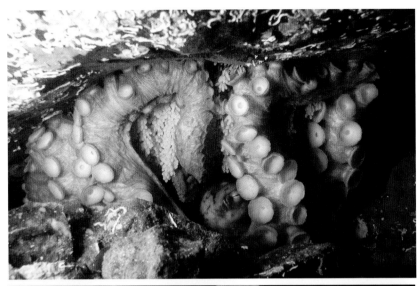

Top: Egg clusters, attached to the roof of the den, dangle like bunches of grapes within the protective arms of their mother. She grooms and agitates the eggs with her suckers and wards off scavengers.
Photo Neil McDaniel

Bottom: These eggs are ready to hatch. The paralarvae are clearly visible in their now transparent eggs. One egg to the left has hatched and is empty.
Photo Fred Bavendam

Other creatures enter the nest but do not appear to do any damage. These include small worms, snails and crabs such as the longhorn decorator crab (*Chorilia longipes*) and the sharpnose crab (*Scyra acutifrons*).

While the female tends her eggs, she does not feed. We don't know the exact reason for this, but one suggestion is that if the female left the den to hunt, she would leave the eggs unattended and vulnerable to predators. Another suggestion is that the presence of food scraps in or near the den might attract predators. Jim does not subscribe to either of these theories. Because this behaviour is common to many cephalopods, he believes it is more likely linked to an ancestral trait, the reason for which may no longer exist. This is an example of innate behaviour, part of the hard-wired information an octopus is born with.

The development of the embryos depends on the surrounding water temperature. The colder the water, the slower the development; the warmer the water, the faster it proceeds. This is true among most egg-laying marine invertebrates.

Jim has been able to observe much of the development in the wild and develop a time frame for estimating when hatching would occur. If he was lucky enough to have witnessed the egg laying, he would have a pretty accurate idea of how the eggs would look as they developed. In most cases he did not see the egg laying, however, and would have to observe the eggs for signs of development to predict when they would hatch.

WATCHING THE EGGS: A DIVER'S VIEW

Newly laid eggs are glossy white and look like white raindrops. The core that the eggs are woven into is pale green, but within a few weeks the core turns black and remains so.

Two small red dots appear on each egg about 120 to 150 days after the eggs are laid. These dots, the developing eyes of the embryo, are visible through the egg shell. The eggs are no longer as shiny white, and soon one can see the brighter yolk sac in the large end of the egg and the darker developing embryo at the small end.

NO MOTHER COULD GIVE MORE

Once a female giant Pacific octopus has mated, she locates a den suitable for holding her and the eggs she will lay. Eggs are produced one at a time, and their tails are woven together into a string containing an average of 176 eggs. The female glues each completed string to the roof of her den. Eventually she will lay about 390 strings for a total of 68,000 eggs. The female will spend the next 6.5 to 11 months grooming and protecting the eggs. She remains in the den and does not feed for this entire time, resulting in a loss of more than 60 percent of her body weight.

About 180 to 210 days after the eggs are laid, the embryo has used up much of the yolk, and the size of the yolk sac has decreased while the size of the embryo has increased. So that the embryo can continue growing, it moves into the larger portion of the egg. This is actually the second reversal, but it is the only one that a diver can observe.

Over the next few months a diver can watch as the yolk sac becomes smaller and the eggs become darker. Those with sharp eyes may be able to see the movement of the embryo within the egg and the flashing of brown and white colours as the embryo tries out its chromatophores.

About 240 to 270 days after the eggs are laid, hatching occurs.

THE NIGHT OF THE HATCH

It might seem logical that the eggs would hatch over the same period of time and in the same order as they were laid. This does happen in many octopuses, including the giant Pacific octopus, but not always. Jim has witnessed a number of hatchings in which he has seen the nest intact one day and completely hatched out the next morning.

Top: The yolk sacs of these paralarvae are clearly visible as the white portion at the bulbous end of the egg. These eggs are about 150 to 180 days old. Photo Neil McDaniel

Bottom: Most of these paralarvae have undergone reversal, and the white yolk sac is now visible in the narrow portion of the egg. These eggs are between 180 and 210 days old and still more than a month away from hatching. Photo Neil McDaniel

Jim collected strings of unhatched eggs from time to time and took them to his lab. When observing the eggs through a dissecting microscope, he found that the water surrounding the eggs was warmed by the microscope lights, often causing the eggs to hatch. He probably collected strings of eggs that had not been laid at the same time, yet even eggs from different strings hatched nearly simultaneously.

Some type of chemical released from a hatched egg stimulates other eggs to hatch as well, Jim suspected. The embryos often had different amounts of food remaining in the yolk sac below their mouth. In some cases the yolk sac was consumed, but in others the yolk sac was still large enough that the paralarva had to bite it off. Clearly some of the paralarvae were not as well developed as others but were able to survive even if they hatched somewhat prematurely.

The hatch normally occurs at night. It may start at dusk, but often it is several hours after dark before things really get underway. As the eggs hatch in ever-increasing numbers, the female blows strongly onto the strings of eggs, causing them to thrash around. This helps the paralarvae to pop out of the eggs and aids in flushing them away from the den.

MOTHER'S JOB IS DONE

In most cases the female survives the hatching and lingers in the den for another few weeks before she dies. During the entire nesting period, which may have dragged on as long as 11 months, the female has not eaten. By hatching time she has lost more than 60 percent of her body weight, sometimes as much as 85 percent! Even though the eggs have hatched the female continues to "mother" them as before. She grooms the hatched-out egg cases even though the paralarvae are long gone.

Experiments have been done in which the eggs have been removed from the ovary of a mated female. Incredibly the female went through the entire egg laying and grooming process, even though she had no eggs or nest. This "phantom nesting" shows that a behavioural lock and key is triggered at sexual maturity or at mating.

Above: Jim collects egg strings from a hatched nest. The strings will be examined for unhatched eggs, external parasites and den cohabitants, and then counted to get an estimate of how many eggs were laid.
Photo Fred Bavendam

Opposite top: Just minutes old, these paralarvae are stubby-armed versions of their parents. In the wild, the paralarvae would swim to the surface of the ocean where they would spend up to 10 months as part of the plankton. Photo Fred Bavendam

Opposite bottom: In a laboratory setting, warming water temperatures cause a cluster of giant Pacific octopus eggs to hatch. A newly hatched paralarva is visible at right; just below it, another struggles to squeeze free of its egg. Photo Fred Bavendam

In some cases the female does not have enough energy stored to survive the whole nesting period and dies before the eggs hatch. Usually her last act is to vacate the den and crawl away. She usually only moves a metre or two before she dies. Again there is no solid evidence on why the female vacates the den, but Jim subscribes to the theory that if the female died in the den her decomposing body could foul the water and attract scavengers. One can understand that females not leaving the den might have resulted, in an evolutionary sense, in the nest being discovered and eaten. This would result in the failure of her genes to be passed on to successive generations. The genes that were passed on would be those of females who successfully distracted predators away from the nest.

While this strategy is interesting, it is not totally successful. In several cases where the female died before the eggs hatched, even though the embryos developed properly, the eggs did not hatch. Without the agitation provided by the female blowing water over them, the closely packed eggs remain immobile and pressed against each other. As a result the paralarvae are unable to force their way out of the eggs, and most perish.

Jim found it sad to observe nests where only a partial hatch was successful. As he counted strings and eggs, he often found thousands of dead paralarvae. Sometimes nature seemed harsh and wasteful.

Here's a breakdown of the nesting process:

Event	Number of Days
Egg laying observed	0
Egg laying complete	28–42
Eyes observed	120–150
Second reversal observed	180–210
Hatching observed	240–270
Female dies	220–330

IT'S A BIG NEW WORLD, AND A DANGEROUS ONE

For those paralarvae that hatch successfully, the challenges of survival are beyond daunting. At hatching they weigh an average of 25.3 mg (0.0009 oz), about the weight of 1.4 grains of converted white rice. The first thing the paralarvae do is swim from the nesting den to the ocean surface more than 20 m (66 ft) above. Many of the paralarvae will not even survive that initial journey, as rockfishes, greenlings and perch—the first of many hungry predators the paralarvae will face—often hover around the den.

On the surface, the paralarvae cling to the underside of the surface by surface tension and become part of the plankton (drifting organisms). For the next seven to ten months they move at the mercy of the currents. They drop off the surface to feed and then swim back up to rest. During this time they are vulnerable to myriad predators that feed on plankton, including everything from pulsing sea jellies to mighty blue whales.

At a weight of approximately three to five grams (0.10 to 0.18 oz), the paralarvae become too heavy for surface tension to support, and the miniature octopuses drop to the ocean floor to begin life as benthic organisms (creatures that live on the ocean bottom). Even this trip is not without risk, as the paralarvae may have drifted out into the deep ocean. If they end up in water more than 2,000 m (6,600 ft) deep, the paralarvae are unlikely to survive.

QUESTIONS AND ANSWERS

Of the average of 68,000 eggs that are laid, you may wonder, how many actually survive to reproduce? The answer is that if a female survives to hatching, almost all the eggs will hatch.

Now we have to change our thinking from individual animals to all the animals of a breeding group. A breeding group is called a population; for the sake of an example, think of all the humans on earth as a population. Any population of plants or animals needs to replace only the parents to have a stable population. For example, if all human parents have two children, the world's population remains stable. We know that some families have no children, however, while others have numerous children. The net result is that humans are producing far more individuals than are dying, and our population is therefore increasing.

Opposite: Few giant Pacific octopuses survive to die of old age, but their fate is still to become part of the food chain. Here a sunflower sea star (*Pycnopodia helianthoides*) scavenges octopus remains. Sea stars and crabs will completely dispose of the rest within a few days, leaving only the two portions of the beak to mark its passing. Photo Jim Cosgrove

In other animal populations, including many that are losing habitat, the reproductive adults are not replacing themselves, and the population is gradually decreasing. The current evidence suggests that the giant Pacific octopus population is stable. That means that out of the 68,000 eggs that hatched, only two would be expected to survive and reproduce.

What happens to the male after mating? This is a more difficult question, as we have little solid evidence. We do know that males grow to be heavier and larger than females and continue to feed after mating.

From a previous study Jim was able to show that the growth rate of both males and females is about 1 percent per day, roughly a doubling of body weight every 80 days. This rate slows as the animals get larger, and beyond about 20 kg (44 lb) they double their body weight every 100 to 120 days or roughly every four months.

Most of the mature males found are under 40 kg (88 lb). Given that they were the same weight as the females when they reached sexual maturity at approximately 15 to 18 kg (33 to 40 lb), then for a male to grow to 40 kg would only take another five or six months. That would mean that the males are dying at about 38 months or just over three years of age. It also means that the male giant Pacific octopuses die younger than the females. Note that these data apply only to southern BC. Colder waters such as those of Alaska, Russia, Korea and northern Japan likely delay maturation, and giant octopuses there may be one or perhaps two years older when they die.

When we find the bodies of deceased males, an examination of the remains shows that there are seldom any mature spermatophores in the gonads. The dissection of healthy male giant Pacific octopuses shows that they hold 10 or fewer mature spermatophores at any one time. The assumption—not yet proven—is that when a male uses up his stock of spermatophores, he has reached the end of his life.

The male becomes, in human terms, senile (the proper term for octopuses is senescent), and his behaviour can become very erratic and unpredictable. Jim and many other divers have encountered large male giant Pacific octopuses prowling around in the daytime. Sometimes they will stride over the bottom and even follow you up into the water column in an effort to contact you. This certainly can get your attention if you are grabbed by a big octopus that you did not see coming. Clearly this is not normal behaviour and could be fatal if a seal or sea lion discovered the octopus. In fact this is likely the fate of some male octopuses when they become senescent.

This unusual behaviour has resulted in more than one diver relating stories of being grabbed or chased out of the water by an aggressive giant Pacific octopus. Jim has had a couple of noteworthy experiences.

The first was during a dive in shallow Telegraph Bay near Victoria. Jim had been hunting octopuses for display at Sealand of the Pacific and had already visited several sites with no success. The seas had picked up, and the boat was starting to take a pounding. Telegraph Bay was a last resort, as it was out of the prevailing wind but too shallow to have any big animals. Some small octopuses would be better than nothing, he decided. Jim and his buddy Paul Rankin dropped into the water only to find horrible visibility. They started off as a team but quickly became separated as they searched. Every few minutes they would bump into each other as they worked toward the entrance to the bay.

Finally Jim felt a firm hand on his shoulder and thought his partner had found him again. As he started to turn, several rubbery arms and some webbing wrapped around his head and shoulders, and it was quickly apparent that a hefty octopus had accosted him. He secured his vital air regulator with both hands and forced his head down into the mud bottom as much as he could. After a few minutes of prodding and pulling, the octopus let go and retreated. At that point Jim was able to capture it, and they delivered a 29 kg (64 lb) male giant Pacific octopus to Sealand. It was only in later years that he was able to understand why a male octopus was active in the daytime in such shallow, turbid water.

A second incident happened many years later. Jim was diving with two others from his research team—David Gagliardi and Leah Saville—at a den where they suspected a mating was taking place. A large male octopus was sitting quietly outside a den where they had seen a female nesting in previous years. A quick check of the den confirmed that there was another octopus inside, and they suspected that it was a female. While Saville and Jim watched the male and the den, Gagliardi moved slightly deeper to check another known den. His hand signals indicated that this den was also occupied.

Immediately after Gagliardi peered into the lower den, the octopus emerged and bolted out so aggressively that Gagliardi moved off to a nearby ridge about five metres (16 ft) away. The octopus turned out to be a large male estimated to be about 30 kg (66 lb). It crawled purposefully toward Gagliardi with both front arms fully extended toward him. This forced Gagliardi to swim up off the reef and into open water. Undeterred, the octopus vaulted off the bottom and followed. Gagliardi ascended even more but the giant Pacific octopus was still in hot pursuit. Eventually it dropped to the bottom and gave up on catching Gagliardi, but by this time it had seen the other two divers and started down the slope toward them.

As it approached them it noticed the other male, veered away and continued down the slope. The male at the entrance to the den did not react at all.

The Octopus at Home

The remarkable behaviours of giant Pacific octopuses make them intriguing creatures. Jim's personal fascination has led him to spend more than 30 years studying them, and he is always excited to find a den and have a chance to interact with one. Sometimes octopuses are fearful and cower in the den, ignoring him or even blowing water through the funnel toward him. Other octopuses tentatively reach out with one or two arms to touch and taste him. Then there are the bold, aggressive octopuses that emerge in a flurry from the den and pursue him across the bottom and even up into the water column. Every dive is different, and every encounter offers a potential lifetime memory.

THERE'S NO PLACE LIKE HOME

Giant Pacific octopuses are benthic creatures once they descend from the plankton layer. Their need upon settling—and for the rest of their lives—is to find or create a den that will provide them with a protective home.

When giant Pacific octopuses first settle, they are as big as the end of your thumb. They weigh about four grams (0.14 oz) and are usually less than two centimetres (0.79 in) in total body length.

Above: This diminutive giant Pacific octopus has likely just settled to the bottom from the plankton layer, where it has been living for the past seven to ten months. It will now have to learn how to catch small shrimps and crabs while avoiding a new gauntlet of predators. Photo Mike Kalina

Opposite: The Pacific red octopus frequently makes its home in a discarded man-made object such as a broken beer bottle. The bottle makes an easy-to-defend den and provides a good nesting site. Small giant Pacific octopuses also make homes in bottles and jars but quickly outgrow them. Photo Mike Kalina

Such small morsels are tasty snack food for fishes such as black-eyed gobies and small rockfishes. Indeed they are vulnerable to many invertebrate carnivores such as sea anemones, prawns, crabs and even worms. At this size they select dens that provide maximum protection, so even man-made items like narrow-necked glass bottles are popular hideouts. Pacific red octopuses also use glass bottles for homes, and thus old garbage dumps can be an excellent place to look for these small octopuses and juvenile giant Pacific octopuses.

Small octopuses sometimes disappear from sight simply by using their front arms to push up a pile of sediment in front of them and then slipping into the hole and allowing the muck to cover them. In a few seconds they vanish from view, leaving only the eyes exposed.

When Jim first started diving along the coast of BC, he discovered that certain dens hosted an octopus time after time. Other potential dens were usually empty or were only occupied once in a while. He also found that a giant Pacific octopus would sometimes modify a previously used den or excavate an entirely new den close to one that had been used frequently over the years. Why was this? What made a certain den so desirable, while octopuses never selected other apparently satisfactory sites? Were dens that were easily seen from a distance selected more often? These sites included dens under tall rocks, or rocks with anemones on them, rather than inconspicuous rocks.

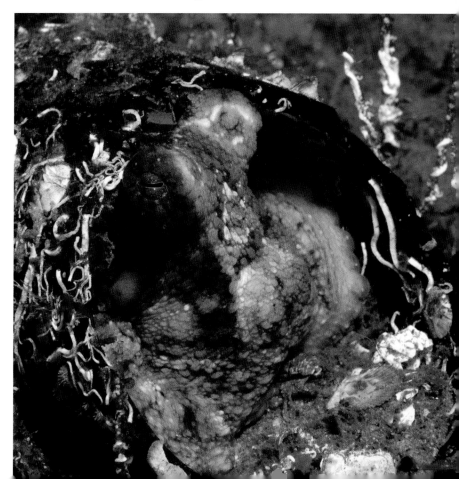

As part of a three-year study, Jim looked at all the variables involved in each den where he found an octopus that weighed more than 2.5 kg (5.5 lb). He considered variables such as the depth of water, the temperature of the water at the den entrance, the presence of other octopuses in the area and the distance to their dens, the substrate surrounding the den (sand, mud, shell, rubble or rocks), the appearance of the outside of the den (under the largest rock in the area or a rock covered by plumose anemones), the number of entrances into the den, the shape of the entrances (vertical or horizontal cracks, excavated dens), the height off the bottom (on vertical rock faces, for example) and the internal volume of the den, which proved to be very difficult to measure accurately. In short Jim looked at everything he thought an octopus would see, touch, taste or experience when it selected a den.

The results of the study were surprising. Although all the factors he assessed are likely considered by an octopus selecting a home, the internal volume of the den usually proves to be the decisive factor. Larger octopuses select larger dens and smaller octopuses select smaller dens. There may be other factors that a giant Pacific octopus regards as value-added features, but the internal volume of the den trumps other factors even if it means excavating a new den close to a well-used existing den.

Since giant Pacific octopuses grow so quickly, an animal can occupy a particular den for only a short time before it must move on to more spacious accommodations. In another study Jim confirmed that these octopuses are exceedingly transient. Even if they hang around the same area, they will move from one den to another and may even have multiple dens.

Dens vary according to the habitat that the octopus lives in. In areas where sunken logs have become buried in soft mud, an octopus will excavate a hole under a log, and a female may attach her eggs to the log overhead. When young, a giant Pacific octopus may also use human refuse as a den.

The sand flats at Dungeness, Washington, offer a significant source of food—Dungeness crabs—but have a distinct lack of den sites. This allows octopus fishers to employ a fishing method that has been used in the Mediterranean for thousands of years.

They place wooden traps on the sand flats near the crab beds, and the giant Pacific octopuses simply crawl into the traps to use them as snacking spots to eat a couple of crabs before continuing on a hunting trip. Commercial prawn and crab fishers often find octopuses inside their traps when the trapline is pulled up.

Researchers in Prince William Sound, Alaska, have described giant Pacific octopus dens of two types. The first is the conventional den amid rocks at depths below 20 m (66 ft). The second is above the waterline when the tide goes out. The octopus excavates a den under a large boulder where it can remain bathed in cool water when the tide recedes. Native Americans in Alaska and—as demonstrated by Nuu-chah-nulth and Coast Salish oral histories and artifacts in the Royal BC Museum—First Nations people in BC have long used variations of a hooked stick to capture them. People of the Haida First Nation still use this method of octopus harvesting.

You might ask why giant Pacific octopuses in Alaska would live in the intertidal zone. It is certainly not as common in the rest of the giant Pacific octopus's range. The answer comes in a cute bundle of the world's most luxurious fur: the sea otter. In northern and remote parts of Alaska sea otters survived the fur trading

As cute and cuddly as sea otters (*Enhydra lutris*) appear, these voracious eaters can have profound effects on marine ecosystems, consuming large quantities of sea urchins, gastropods and clams.
Photo Jim Cosgrove

era, while those from southern Alaska south to California were very nearly exterminated. Where sea otters live, the giant Pacific octopus population falls into two segments. One group lives above two metres (six feet) in the intertidal zone, and the other lives below 20 m (66 ft). At depths between, sea otters are a major predator and will certainly take any octopus they find.

Clearly there is no such thing as a typical giant Pacific octopus den. These creatures will use whatever nature provides and modify it to meet their needs.

HAVE A BITE

When giant Pacific octopus paralarvae hatch and ascend to the surface, they become part of the plankton, the drifters of the ocean. Plankton is split into two components: the plants are called phytoplankton, and the animals are known as zooplankton. The octopus paralarvae are part of the zooplankton. Some zooplankton such as copepods feed mostly on the phytoplankton. Octopus paralarvae are carnivores right from the start, however, and hunt the zooplankton portion of the plankton. Animals

Dozens of shells of swimming scallops (*Chlamys* species) are piled outside this giant Pacific octopus's den. These succulent bivalves are extremely abundant in some parts of the Gulf Islands of southwestern BC. Photo Neil McDaniel

such as copepods, mysids and the larvae of many other species are potential prey. As the paralarvae grow, larger zooplankton and larval forms of many fishes may appear on their menu. Much of this is speculation, because little scientific work has been done in the field. Our knowledge is based on what is found in the plankton with octopus paralarvae and what few successes there have been in raising octopus paralarvae in captivity.

Once the paralarvae settle to the bottom, the octopuses seek larger prey such as small shrimps and crabs.

In their 1996 book *Cephalopod Behaviour*, R.T. Hanlon and J.B. Messenger describe the seven ways in which cephalopods obtain food. These include ambushing, luring, stalking, pursuing, speculative hunting, hunting in disguise and co-operative hunting.

Giant Pacific octopuses are known to use four of these seven methods. They are not generally ambush hunters, but they are certainly not reluctant to snag an unwary crab that saunters past the front of a den. Jim has worked with many film crews that obtained footage of octopuses feeding by having a diver drop a crab near the den entrance.

Dr. Roland Anderson of the Seattle Aquarium has some excellent video footage—on the internet for some years now—of a giant Pacific octopus that discovered that dogfishes are tasty and not very bright. The octopus can be seen sitting at the bottom of a large aquarium while dogfish and other fishes go about their

WHO'S FOR DINNER?

Octopuses are opportunistic feeders and will take any food easily available to them, but they do have preferences and will pass up some food for another more favoured prey. As paralarvae they feed on small creatures such as mysid shrimp, copepods, euphausids and larval forms of many other animals. Once the octopuses settle to the bottom, they start to hunt a new group of prey, including small crustaceans such as tiny shrimp and crabs. As the octopuses increase in size, they select larger foods including crabs, scallops and bivalves such as cockles and clams. Given the opportunity, octopuses can even capture fishes and birds.

A giant Pacific octopus with champagne tastes. This gourmet mollusc appears to prefer pinto abalone (*Haliotis kamtschatkana*), a tasty shellfish nearly wiped out by commercial fisheries and poaching.
Photo Fred Bavendam

business. Then, as a dogfish passes close by, the octopus quickly reaches out and grabs it with the front pairs of arms while staying anchored to the bottom with the rear pairs. The dogfish is quickly enveloped in the web, where it is subdued and eventually eaten. This happened on several occasions, but not until a video camera was left recording at night were aquarium workers able to identify the culprit. To view this remarkable behaviour, try an internet search for "octopus and dogfish."

Giant Pacific octopuses are most commonly speculative hunters, and their strategy generally takes one of two forms. Typically an octopus crawls along using the tips of the front two pairs of arms to probe into cracks and crevices in the rocks where a tasty crab might be hiding. When it locates prey, the octopus latches on with its suckers, extracts it from the crack and tucks it under the folds of the interbrachial web.

Another form of speculative hunting is simply to move over areas such as mud flats where food has been found before. In this case the speculative hunting may turn into stalking and pursuit if the prey is in the open and attempting escape.

A possible example of speculative hunting can be seen in a video of a ROV (remotely operated vehicle) that a giant Pacific octopus "attacked." It is likely that this octopus was out hunting and happened to see the ROV. To taste the vehicle it had to touch it, and the operators of the ROV interpreted that as an attack. The vehicle's thrusters blasted the octopus away,

NOT SO FUSSY

While giant Pacific octopuses seem to prefer certain kinds of prey—including crabs, scallops and clams—the scrap piles at their den entrances have revealed a wide range of species consumed, among them 19 species of bivalves, six species of snails, seven species of crabs and a half-dozen types of fishes.

but its taste of the ROV convinced it that the machine was not food and it never returned. To see the video, search the internet for "octopus and ROV."

Yet a third form of speculative hunting is rarely seen in giant Pacific octopuses, but Jim has been fortunate enough to witness it while diving at the Ogden Point breakwater in Victoria. In this "web over" form of hunting, the octopus pounces onto a rock and completely envelopes it with the umbrella-like web between its arms. It then uses the tips of its arms to probe under the rock to see if it can flush out a fish or crab. If this is not successful, it will move on and pounce on the next rock that attracts its attention.

One of the most fascinating examples of speculative hunting came from a report about a giant Pacific octopus that briefly lived under a rock near a Washington State Ferries dock. The rock was exposed at low tide, and the giant Pacific octopus had somehow discovered that seagulls occasionally landed on the rock. Ferry workers observed that every few minutes an octopus arm would emerge from the water and wander around on the top of the rock. When it encountered the leg of a bird, it seized the unsuspecting gull and yanked it into the water where it was presumably drowned and consumed.

Below a dock on Quadra Island, a small giant Pacific octopus has discovered a dogfish (*Squalus acanthias*) dumped overboard by a local fisher. These octopuses are opportunists and will scavenge food that they have not killed. The photographer removed the dogfish from the octopus several times and each time it returned to claim its prize. Photo Fred Bavendam

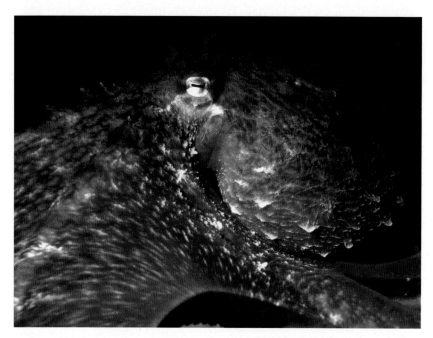

Above: When hunting, the giant Pacific octopus crawls over the bottom, probing around rocks with its foremost arms. When it tastes prey it pounces forward with the arms and web spread wide like an umbrella to snare crabs that might be hiding near the rocks. Photo Neil McDaniel

Opposite top: While giant Pacific octopuses commonly feed on crabs, the Puget Sound king crab (*Lopholithodes mandtii*) is not usually on the menu. Only in rare circumstances will an octopus tackle one of these heavily armoured beasts. Photo Neil McDaniel

Opposite bottom: The Puget Sound king crab has a tough exoskeleton, but a moulting crab has a softer shell that may make it vulnerable to a large and hungry octopus. Photo Neil McDaniel

Octopuses use stalking and pursuing methods when prey is located in an open area. When the area is large and escape is unlikely, then the octopus may jet up into the water, descend on top of a crab and scoop it up in its web. If the crab sees it coming and flees, the octopus may swim alongside until it is ready to pounce. Where bivalves such as heart cockles are a major food source rather than crabs, the octopus can move along in the eelgrass beds to hunt, grabbing cockles before they have a chance to dig to safety.

Giant Pacific octopuses vary widely in the kinds of prey they prefer. In some areas they specialize in crabs such as red rock crabs, Dungeness crabs or kelp crabs. In others their prey are bivalves such as heart cockles or swimming scallops. Some octopuses develop a taste for a specific food. For example, some middens consist only of swimming scallop shells while others contain exclusively abalone shells. Even though other tasty prey such as red rock crabs were available, they were not taken.

An octopus may use several different techniques to eat a hard-shelled creature. They may physically pull it apart using the suckers, bite it open using the sharp beak or drill through the shell using the toothed radula. Prey that are difficult to pull apart, such as clams, often have holes drilled in them by the radula; then the octopus introduces salivary secretions to paralyze and dissolve the connective tissues of the prey.

One of the major problems in the scientific study of giant Pacific octopuses is that they are planktonic when they hatch,

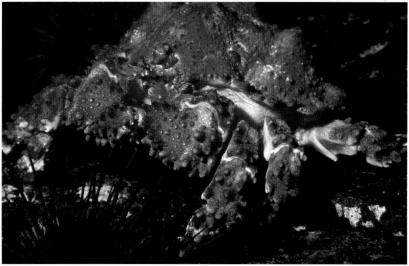

Above: Midden remains at this giant Pacific octopus den show a strong preference for red rock crabs (*Cancer productus*). Some octopuses seem to prefer these tasty crustaceans over any other prey, while others favour scallops or clams. Photo Brandon Cole

Opposite: Oblivious to the predator lurking in the cave behind them, a group of striped shrimp *(Pandalus danae)* pick through the table scraps in front of an octopus den. Photo Jim Cosgrove

and that phase lasts for up to ten months. As part of the plankton drifting in the ocean, the paralarvae are very hard to track. Why doesn't someone just hatch some eggs and raise the paralarvae in captivity, where they can easily be observed? This is much easier to say than to do. It has been tried a number of times with little success for a number of reasons. Years ago the Vancouver Aquarium tried to raise some paralarvae, for example, but one evening the water supply pump failed, and they all died.

Another aquarium facility brought in a mixture of plankton with the idea that the paralarvae would select what they wanted and ignore the rest. Unfortunately some of the plankton recognized the octopus paralarvae as food, and the project was consumed before the bad guys could be sorted out from the good guys.

Those who have an aquarium know about the many problems that have to be considered. Temperature, light-dark cycles, salinity, ammonia, filter types and other physical parameters are challenges that must be overcome. The big issue appears to be food. What do the paralarvae eat, how much food is enough and how do food preferences change as the paralarvae grow?

To our knowledge there has been only one successful rearing of a giant Pacific octopus from egg to adult. That took place at the Seattle Aquarium under the watchful eye of Susan Snyder. She successfully raised one male to a 29 kg (64 lb) adult, which died at the age of three years and two months. That she managed to raise one was a significant success, but considering that she started with more than 50,000 eggs, you can appreciate how difficult it was. There is just so much that we do not know.

What is clear is that the paralarvae feed on the zooplankton that drifts with them. Once the paralarvae settle, they switch to larger food such as small shrimps and crabs and perhaps soft-bodied prey that leave no remains in the midden.

VERY TOUCHING AND TASTY TOO

The suckers of an octopus are able to taste what they touch. This ability, called chemotaxis, allows the octopus to hunt in areas where it cannot see, such as under rocks and in complete darkness. In encounters between divers and giant Pacific octopuses, divers often fail to realize that when the giant Pacific octopus reaches out to touch them, it is also tasting them to see if they are edible. Given the strength of a giant Pacific octopus, divers should not allow octopuses to contact them unless they're prepared to deal with a potential confrontation.

For many years it was thought that giant Pacific octopuses hunted only at night and then snoozed in their dens all day, digesting the food captured the previous evening. Dr. Jennifer Mather from the University of Lethbridge, Alberta, led a month-long project to verify this nocturnal feeding behaviour, and Jim participated in the study. During the day, divers located one or more octopuses in their dens. Each animal was captured, weighed, sexed and tagged with an electronic tag. Then it was returned to its den and released. Every 15 minutes the location of the octopus was obtained and plotted onto a chart of the research area.

Much to their surprise, the researchers found that the octopuses moved as much during the day as they did at night. The tracking turned into a round-the-clock ordeal for the next 28 days. On average the octopuses made six trips greater than 20 m (66 ft) every 24 hours.

The results of this study dispelled several popular notions. The Giant Pacific octopuses moved—presumably hunting—as much in the day as they did at night, although the night excursions tended to be longer than the day ones. The average trip covered 110 to 120 m (363 to 400 ft) and took about 60 minutes during the day and 90 minutes at night.

Octopuses are preyed upon by many fishes, including lingcod *(Ophiodon elongatus)*. A voracious predator with a mouthful of needle-sharp teeth, this lingcod is in the process of gulping down a hapless octopus.
Photo Mike Kalina

Each giant Pacific octopus had an average range of a square about 230 m (760 ft) per side. There is a difference between a range and a territory; a range is shared with others of the same species, while a territory is usually exclusive to an individual or a family group, for example a pride of lions. The ranges of the tagged octopuses overlapped up to 94 percent, and only once were two octopuses recorded in the same place at the same time. Most of the time the animals were not closer than 50 m (165 ft).

RUNNING THE GAUNTLET

A parallel challenge to the search for food is to avoid becoming dinner for something else. In the ocean it is a common fate to be eaten by something. Almost nothing dies of old age except the apex species such as whales.

When the hatched paralarvae become part of the plankton, they are subject to all the hazards of being totally exposed in the open ocean. The paralarvae are food for other large drifters such as jellyfishes, ctenophores and siphonophores. They also are easy pickings for the swimming animals such as fishes and the largest of the plankton feeders in our area, the great whales and basking sharks. While the paralarvae are in the plankton, untold millions of them are consumed.

Once they settle, juvenile giant Pacific octopuses become prey for a completely different set of predators. Some, such as the sea anemones, simply sit and wait for the unwary to blunder into them. Active hunters such as clam worms, crabs, large shrimps and many fishes may also eat any small octopus they encounter. Predation from the air now becomes an issue, with birds such as

Above: A young lingcod (*Ophiodon elongatus*) has caught a small giant Pacific octopus but is unable to swallow it. The octopus has reached through the gills of the lingcod and grasped the sides of the fish. While the final outcome of this encounter went unobserved, the authors speculate that the octopus escaped, likely with some damage to the lingcod.
Photo Don Coleman

Opposite: Giant Pacific octopuses have been seen capturing seagulls near the water's edge, but a bald eagle (*Haliaeetus leucocephalus*) turned the tables when it grabbed a small octopus from the shallows near Hornby Island. Photo Kevin Harman

bald eagles, osprey and great blue herons fishing the shallows. Larger octopuses also eat smaller octopuses; cannibalism is common in the ocean.

As the octopus matures and becomes larger, the variety of predators decreases but their size increases. Predators now include larger fishes such as lingcod and halibut as well as river otters, sea otters, harbour seals and sea lions. It is likely that marine mammals such as dolphins and porpoises, given the opportunity, also feed on octopuses. There are many reports of squid beaks—though not octopus beaks—being found in the stomachs of dolphins and porpoises. Jim has witnessed harbour seals feeding on octopuses at the surface, and others have reported finding octopus beaks in the stomachs of sea lions and fur seals.

Giant Pacific octopuses do their best to avoid confrontations with predators. They make the majority of their longer hunting trips at night, when most visual predators are at a disadvantage. Notable exceptions are harbour seals and sea lions, which do hunt at night. When out in the open, octopuses keep a careful watch for moving shadows and try to remain near cover. They camouflage, changing both colour and skin texture to match their surroundings so that they're not detected. If threatened they turn all of their suckers downward, since the white sucker disks do not have chromatophores and therefore cannot change colour. Lastly, they stop breathing or drastically reduce their respiration so that the white of the inside of their gill slits does not flash. The inside of the mantle around the gill slits also lacks chromatophores and cannot be camouflaged except by keeping it closed.

Giant Pacific octopuses need to breathe, and every breath is important. Stopping breathing for any length of time is very

Steller sea lions (*Eumetopias jubatus*) are significant predators of giant Pacific octopuses, especially during the pupping and breeding season in May and June, when octopuses make up nearly half their diet. Photo Neil McDaniel

stressful and cannot be maintained for more than two or three minutes, but it is an essential tactic in avoiding detection. On occasion Jim has known an octopus was in the area—but could not see it. By just sitting and waiting a few seconds he has sometimes been able to spot the octopus once it started to breathe again and the white of the gill slits flashed against the dark background.

When an octopus meets a predator, it has a number of options, depending on where it is at the time—in a den or out in the open—and what the predator is.

If the octopus is in a den, its options include retreating farther into the den and blocking the entrance with the front pairs of arms. The rear pairs of arms can lock onto the rock so that the octopus cannot be pulled out. The octopus is even prepared to lose an arm or two in the struggle, but it is unlikely to lose its life if it can remain in the den. Even if found in the open, it does its best to grip the bottom with all of its suckers so that it cannot be pulled off.

When confronted by a predator while out in the open, the octopus has several options. If the predator is some distance away, the octopus may simply lift up off the bottom slightly and jet away so the predator is no longer in visual range. Then it may look for a defensive position or retreat to a rocky crevice or hole.

If the octopus decides the predator would see it if it moved, then it may change colour and skin texture to match its background, turn all its suckers downward and stop breathing briefly until the predator has passed by. If it can glide under a blade of kelp or into a crack or crevice in the rocks, so much the better.

If the octopus is certain it has been detected by the predator, it may change colour and texture, including forming a large single false eye in the centre of its head above the first pair of arms and below the eyes. This false eye, called a frontal white spot, may convince the predator to move on. The octopus may also use its funnel to blow water at the predator or spread itself out wide and abruptly blanch white in an effort to make itself look as large and intimidating as possible and scare off the attacker.

This giant Pacific octopus has suffered a nasty wound, which has healed over leaving a white scar. Photo Neil McDaniel

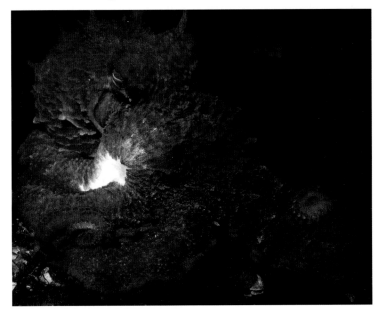

Above: Aware that it has been discovered, a giant Pacific octopus blanches white with a contrasting dark bar across the eye in a last-ditch attempt to frighten the intruder away. This abrupt and striking colour change, including the formation of a false eye, can be effective in scaring off predators.
Photo Neil McDaniel

Opposite: Kevin Van Cleemput watches a giant Pacific octopus stride over the bottom in Saanich Inlet. Observed from a comfortable distance, an octopus will sometimes go about its business heedless of nearby divers.
Photo Neil McDaniel

Lastly, the octopus may jet away, sometimes also ejecting ink via the funnel directly at the predator. This is a last resort, as it has given up the security of being in contact with the bottom. If the predator catches it, the octopus can be dragged to the surface and eaten or perhaps swallowed whole by a large fish.

Giant Pacific octopuses are like most cephalopods in having an amazing ability to regenerate lost parts. If an arm is damaged or lost in conflict, the part is rapidly repaired or replaced. Interestingly, the nerves of a lost limb are also replaced, so that the suckers function as normal. This regenerative ability is currently of interest to human researchers involved in the study of human nerve regeneration. The inability of the human nervous system to repair nerve damage is a major concern. Perhaps the humble invertebrates can provide the breakthrough clues to stimulating nerve regeneration in humans.

When contacted by a predator, the giant Pacific octopus strives to protect itself. Most octopuses have never seen a diver before and likely view one as a potential predator. If a diver rushes in and grabs an octopus, it will anchor itself to the bottom and latch onto the diver with its front pairs of arms. If it gets an arm on a diver's regulator or mask, it can displace these and create a very serious situation. We urge divers to view a giant Pacific octopus from a distance. If you are going to approach one, do so very slowly so that it has the opportunity to get past the fight-or-flight response and get to the curious stage.

Skilled divers have found that they can encourage an octopus to move by slowly edging into its personal space. We've all experienced someone standing too close, which makes us want to move away to a more comfortable distance. Octopuses also seem to have a personal space. If you get too close to them, they cling to the bottom and prepare to defend themselves. If you are

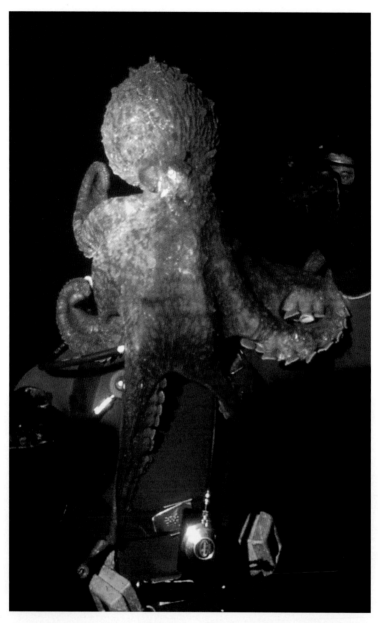

A considerable source of amusement for his buddies, this diver could still get into serious trouble if the curious giant Pacific octopus gets a grip on his mask and regulator. Unless you have previous training, we recommend against allowing an octopus to climb over your head. Photo Doug Pemberton

experienced with giant Pacific octopuses, you can place yourself at just the right distance to stimulate an animal but not frighten it. Then you must remain motionless and out of reach. Once it gets over the initial fright response, it will likely start to crawl away. You can then move toward it, but you must maintain the same distance between yourself and the octopus. Eventually the octopus will start to move more quickly and may lift off the bottom and start to swim. At this point the octopus is no longer in contact with the bottom, and you can move in much closer to view the animal or to take pictures.

The bottom line is that a diver should never touch a giant Pacific octopus unless prepared for what might follow.

HOW DO I LOOK NOW?

Octopus skin contains millions of specialized pigment cells called chromatophores. Octopuses can voluntarily change the texture of their skin to match the texture of their surroundings. This ability to camouflage is directly linked to the behavioural ability to modify their physical appearance to avoid detection or deter a predator.

While giant Pacific octopuses are no slouches at changing colour and texture, they are totally outclassed by a couple of tropical species. The supreme master of mimicry in the octopus world is a very small species found in muddy bays in the waters around Indonesia. When first discovered in the early 1990s, it was undescribed and was known simply as the mimic octopus. Now scientifically described, it is called *Thaumoctopus mimicus*. This name came about from the octopus's ability to imitate the colour, movement and behaviour of other dangerous animals that live in the area. For example, the mimic octopus has been documented imitating a lionfish, which has deadly poisonous spines; a mantis shrimp, with powerful claws that can break bones and shells; a jellyfish, bearing stinging cells; and a banded sea snake, which has fangs and a toxic bite.

This wonderful little octopus drew the attention of divers all over the world. In return the mimic octopus apparently paid attention to the divers it saw, since it has now been documented

Above: The quick-change artist: a series of four frames captured from digital video shows a giant Pacific octopus swimming, then landing on a rocky bottom covered with small white plumose anemones. The octopus changes colour from red to white to blend in with the background in about one-third of a second. Photos Neil McDaniel

Opposite left: What on earth was it doing? This Pacific red octopus was spotted sitting motionless on a sandy bottom, stretched out vertically. One possible answer is that it was trying to mimic one of the orange sea pens which were abundant nearby. Photo Neil McDaniel

Opposite right: Orange sea pens (*Ptilosarcus gurneyi*) can reach 50 cm (20 in) in height and are common on sandy bottoms. Photo Neil McDaniel

Opposite bottom: The mimic octopus (*Thaumoctopus mimicus*), an extraordinary creature that lives in Indo-Pacific regions, gets its name from its amazing ability to imitate the appearance of other marine species such as fish, sea snakes, or in this case, perhaps a sea star. Photo Brandon Cole

The normally shy and retiring southern blue-ringed octopus (*Hapalochlaena maculosa*) is believed to be the most toxic cephalopod in the world. The nocturnal hunter hides during the day under pieces of debris or in discarded bottles in Spencer Gulf, South Australia. Toxin from its bite causes muscular paralysis which can cause a human to stop breathing. Signs posted on many beaches warn about the danger of picking up these potentially deadly octopuses. Photo David Fleetham

walking across the bottom in a bipedal motion using two of its arms as legs. You can watch this if you search the internet for "mimic octopus."

In Australia there is a group of octopuses that are collectively called the blue-ringed octopuses (*Hapalochlaena* species). Members of this group are generally small but have a very potent toxin that has killed people. They are currently thought to be the most toxic cephalopods in the world, and it is not uncommon to find beaches posted with signs warning swimmers and divers to avoid coming in contact with them. The blue-ringed octopus, like many toxic animals, warns by flashing the iridescent blue rings on its skin. This signal is meant to deter a potential predator, but if the warning is not heeded, combat may follow. Then the predator may become the prey if the octopus can get in a successful bite.

Footloose and Smart

The giant Pacific octopus has a number of ways of moving, depending on its needs and the situation.

Crawling is the most common form of locomotion (the act of moving from one place to another). The questions arise: Does the giant Pacific octopus crawl quickly or slowly? How fast is fast, and how slow is slow? Providing an answer in metres per second would be ideal, but that number varies because of the differences in the size of octopuses as they grow. A large octopus with an arm span of three metres can cover the bottom faster than a smaller octopus, at the same speed or slower, depending on its behaviour at the time and what it wants to do.

As an example, consider a giant Pacific octopus that is not feeling threatened and is not hunting. Perhaps it is just moving from one hunting area to another. The front two pairs of legs (arms) are often raised off the bottom and curve back toward the rear of the octopus. The first pair of legs—called L1 and R1—very seldom touch the bottom and appear to be used to balance the octopus as it moves forward. Jim also has a theory—unproven at this time—that the suckers of the raised front pair of legs are constantly tasting the water for hints of what may be approaching and as yet unseen.

Above: Giant Pacific octopuses are not averse to occasional jaunts partially or even fully out of the water. This one takes an afternoon stroll through an eelgrass bed at low tide at Cape Lazo near Comox, BC. Some Alaska octopuses live above the low-tide line and come out to hunt in the eelgrass when the tide comes in. Photo Rick Harbo

Opposite: Giant Pacific octopuses, like most benthic (bottom-dwelling) octopuses, spend most of their hunting time walking across the bottom. The front two pairs of legs are most involved in tasting the water and probing into cracks and crevices, while the rear two pairs of legs provide the push that moves the animal forward. Often the front pairs of legs are held off the bottom, but the rear pairs are almost always in contact with the bottom. Photo Neil McDaniel

The second pair of legs, L2 and R2, occasionally touch the bottom to balance the octopus and aid in moving over obstacles. The third pair of legs, L3 and R3, and the fourth or rear pair of legs, L4 and R4, are the major players in ordinary crawling. They can be seen underneath the octopus's mantle and tend to move only short distances but quite rapidly. They roll forward, grip the bottom and then propel the body of the octopus forward. Working the rear legs in pairs, one pair pushing forward while the other pair is reaching ahead to grip and push, the octopus can move straight forward in a steady and coordinated motion. When an animal is travelling like this, it often has both eyes looking ahead so it can judge distance, but it also moves its eyes back to the side of its head so that it can scan a much wider area to search out cover and perhaps detect predators. The only place the giant Pacific octopus cannot see easily is directly behind itself. To correct for this the octopus occasionally swings its body while walking, which gives it a rearward glimpse.

In the normal crawling mode a giant Pacific octopus can cover hundreds of metres in an hour but still be at minimal risk from predators. It is in contact with the bottom with two pairs of legs and can bring the others into contact with the bottom very quickly if it needs to. It can also camouflage and stop breathing in the wink of an eye. And the octopus has the option of another form of locomotion should the situation require a more urgent avoidance behaviour.

When hunting, an octopus normally crawls, but crawling uses the front two pairs of legs in a different way (see different hunting methods in Chapter Five). It probes under rocks and into crevices with the front pairs of legs; if the suckers taste food, they seize the prey and the legs carry it back to the web and mouth. This much slower form of locomotion is not intended to cover much ground. The octopus remains out of the den only long enough to gather the food it needs and then returns to the den where it has the maximum protection.

In another form of locomotion commonly called jet propulsion, the octopus draws in a mantle-full of water and forces it strongly out through the funnel. When the water is drawn into the mantle, the arms spread out to form an umbrella shape, with the arms as the ribs of the umbrella and the interbrachial web as the material covering the ribs. When water is forced from the mantle, the arms snap together using the web as a bellows to propel the octopus in a particular direction or up into the water column.

A giant Pacific octopus gathers up its arms just before pumping a powerful jet of water from its funnel to start swimming. The double row of suckers along each arm numbers about 200, depending on the age of the animal. Males have fewer because there are no suckers on the end of the hectocotylized arm. Photo Neil McDaniel

Once the octopus is swimming free of the bottom, it curves its second pair of arms into a wing shape, which provides lift just as the curve of a bird's wing does. The other arms trail behind like tails on a kite. The mantle continues to draw water in and pump it out, and the funnel directs the water stream down the length of the arms, allowing the octopus to jet backward while watching to the sides and front to see what is following. The reversed direction may seem strange, but remember that the jetting octopus is actually moving backward and does not see well to the rear. An octopus can also use jet propulsion when hunting to rapidly approach its prey and drop onto it. It can also cover long distances in a short period of time.

Spreading its arms like a wing, a giant Pacific octopus can "fly" considerable distances, propelled by powerful jets of water blown through its funnel. Photo Neil McDaniel

Most commonly jet propulsion is used in an emergency to avoid a predator. If the predator is a visual attacker—one that hunts by sight—quickly disappearing from view is the ideal defence. If the predator is an olfactory predator—one that hunts by smell—rapidly moving across a current might eliminate the scent trail and throw off the predator.

Increased risk and increased metabolic demands are the disadvantages of jet propulsion. The mantle has to work at full strength to draw water in and force it out, and the arms must be held rigidly in the wing formation to provide the lift needed to fly underwater. This extra physical demand taxes the oxygen supply and cannot be maintained, although there is some evidence that a giant Pacific octopus can continue for many minutes like this. If it doesn't avoid a predator with this manoeuvre, it is at great risk of attack, because it is in open water and unable to camouflage as effectively as on the bottom. The octopus is also unable to grasp the bottom and use its strength to prevent it from being dragged to the surface by a predator such as a seal or sea lion.

Once detected, the octopus has one more life-saving tool in its toolbox. Inside the mantle near the interior opening of the funnel are the ink-producing gland and storage sac. The ink sac has a duct that empties into the siphon. If an octopus comes under attack by a predator, or even a perceived predator such as a diver, it can eject multiple large clouds of ink at its attacker. A small giant Pacific octopus is far more likely to discharge ink at a diver than a larger one. Typically a diver approaches from the front—remember the octopus is travelling backward—so the octopus can see the human coming. At the point where contact is possible the animal may pause, assume the open-umbrella formation and then snap all its legs together, shooting backward. At the same time it may blow ink straight at the diver. The octopus does not reform the wing but stays compact like a torpedo and jets backward for one or two breaths. On each breath it discharges another blast of ink that hangs like a dark brown cloud in the water column. After three or four breaths the octopus might completely change direction and head directly toward the bottom, where it can camouflage and grasp the bottom for protection.

In some octopuses the ink has a known effect on the olfactory nerves of the predator. It has been observed that a hunting moray eel released in an aquarium with an octopus and a sufficient quantity of octopus ink is unable to detect the octopus even if it touches the octopus. Once the ink is cleared from the water, the moray will quickly locate and attack the octopus. It is unknown if giant Pacific octopus ink has this affect on any of its predators, but it is unlikely. Since most predators of an adult giant Pacific octopus are visual predators, it is more likely that the ink clouds suspended in the water hide its escape and provide a false target for the predator. Given that the octopus aims ink at the predator's face, it is reasonable to assume that the ink is intended as a visual distraction.

Many octopuses, including giant Pacific octopuses, can move out of the water. Because they no longer have the support of the water and lack a skeleton, their body is pretty much reduced to a slimy-looking blob. The muscular arms and suckers can still function, however, to pull the body along (see aquarium escapes in Chapter Three). In nature it is unusual for giant Pacific octopuses to emerge from the water, but they clearly do. Why they do so is somewhat less clear and is probably a combination of many different reasons.

A series of four frames captured from digital video shows a swimming giant Pacific octopus inking. The concentrated blast of ink expands rapidly and hides the octopus's quick escape. Photos Neil McDaniel

One day while working at the museum, Jim received a most unusual phone call. "Somebody wanted me to drive out to Sidney [north of Victoria] to pick up an octopus off the front lawn of a house. On the way I was wondering how an octopus could possibly have ended up in such a circumstance. Sidney has an active fishing industry, and totes of fishes are moved to town every day. Perhaps an octopus fell out of a fish tote, and someone passing by threw it onto the lawn to get it off the street. Another thought was that maybe the octopus was still alive and had crawled out of a tote before it died. It also crossed my mind that this could be a joke played on the owner by friends or some sort of insult or warning by someone not quite so friendly.

OVERLAND TRAVELS

While sitting out a surface interval between dives in Barkley Sound on the west coast of Vancouver Island, Neil spotted some movement on a small rocky outcrop near the boat. He watched entranced as a nine kilogram (20 lb) giant Pacific octopus emerged from the water and crawled slowly up and over the low-lying reef, transiting more than six metres (20 ft) in the process. Why would an animal adapted to life underwater do this? We don't really know, but it's clear that octopuses are quite capable of travelling for short distances completely out of the water.

"All those musings proved incorrect, as the house was situated on a quiet dead-end cul-de-sac. What was unusual was that the front lawn faced toward the water of Tsehum Harbour. A large, fully mature male giant Pacific octopus had crawled some 12 m [40 ft] out of the water and died on the lawn. Was it senile? Was this the last act of a demented cephalopod? Was it trying to crawl across to another body of water? Did some predator chase it out of the water? We will never know for sure but what is important to understand is that this octopus got there by itself. Its crawl marks were clear on the dewy grass, and there were no other 'footprints' in the grass other than those of the baffled homeowner who had walked out to see what the heck was on her lawn."

In the tropics many species of octopuses have been observed out of the water for quite long times. Several species hunt in tidal pools and cross reef flats to get from one pool to the next. There is even a nocturnal species, which has been observed to emerge from the water and climb into coconut trees in search of coconut crabs.

We should mention that the wonderful website created for the "Pacific Tree Octopus" is a delightful hoax. There is no such creature, although we would be the first to culture it if it did exist. Jim knows the person responsible for the website, who even now has difficulty convincing people that it is just a spoof. There are no terrestrial octopuses known to science anywhere in the world, just as there are no fresh-water octopuses. Octopuses are entirely marine, as far as we know, but nature always seems to have a few surprises up her sleeve.

REMEMBER THIS!

The intelligence of the giant Pacific octopus has long been debated. Designing valid experiments that directly compare its intelligence to that of a dog, cat or a parrot is impossible, given how different these animals are. But we can devise experiments that test whether the giant Pacific octopus can solve problems and learn from previous experiences. The results can help us determine its capabilities as a species.

The online reference source Encyclopedia Britannica states that intelligence is the "mental quality that consists of the abilities to learn from experience, adapt to new situations, understand and handle abstract concepts, and use knowledge to manipulate one's environment."

Some of the elements of the definition such as the comprehension of abstract concepts, and use of knowledge to manipulate the surrounding environment are also coated in other definitions that may or may not apply to cephalopods. How would we know if an octopus or a dog or a cat could understand an abstract concept? The issue of understanding abstract concepts in animals such as octopuses or squids is not one that scientists have an answer for yet. There is some evidence that primates, such as chimpanzees and gorillas, do understand some abstract concepts.

We can, however, look at some of the other elements of the Encyclopedia Britannica's definition if we understand that we humans may be the problem in understanding what is quite clear to the animals themselves.

One issue we need to look at is the difference between innate behaviour and intelligence. Encyclopedia Britannica defines innate behaviour as "involuntary response by an animal to an external

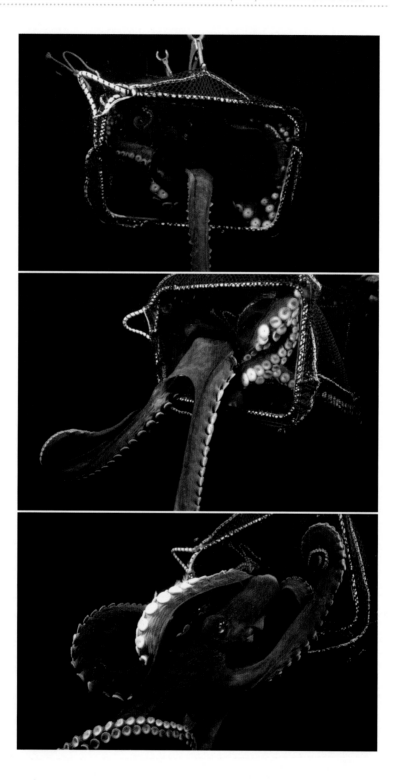

Opposite: An eight-kilogram (18 lb) giant Pacific octopus squeezes through a 5 by 10 cm (2 by 4 in) hole cut into a piece of Plexi-
glas fitted into the mouth of a mesh bag. Although the animal's
arm span was about 1.2 m (4 ft), it easily escaped. In a previous
test by photographer Fred Bavendam, the same octopus was
unable to squeeze through a 5 cm (2 in) circular hole.

Photos Fred Bavendam

stimulus. The concept has come to refer to a complex unlearned
behaviour that is recognizable and predictable in at least one sex
of a species."

Many of the behaviours we observe in giant Pacific octopuses
or other cephalopods are innate behaviours. In fact, because cephalopods do not have parental care to teach them how to hunt
or how to build nests, these behaviours are in the octopus or
squid when it is born and are therefore innate.

So where do we cross the line between innate behaviours
and intelligence? One of the first experiments that gave some
insight into the intelligence of a cephalopod was centred around
a feeding situation. A Mediterranean octopus was given a crab
to eat, but the crab was put inside a glass jar and a cork was put
in the top of the jar to keep the crab in. The cork had a small
hole in it to allow the crab to breathe. When the jar was placed
in the aquarium the octopus did what it would normally do
when food was provided: it pounced on the jar in an attempt to
envelop the crab in its interbrachial web. The octopus encountered only the glass jar, which did not taste like a crab or respond as a crab.

The octopus retreated from the jar and was observed undergo-
ing a series of rapid colour changes while it appeared to study the
problem. It tried several more direct attacks before moving back
to its den in apparent frustration, as indicated by colour changes
and agitated movements. Clearly the octopus had had no previous experience with glass jars and now had a problem to solve.
After some time it ventured out and explored the jar with its front
arms and suckers. It did not attack the jar as before but appeared
to be dealing with the jar rather than the crab. In exploring the
jar, the tip of one of the arms discovered the hole in the cork and

was able to reach down into the jar and touch the crab. At this point, it yanked out the cork, quickly seized the crab and removed it from the jar.

We can credit innate behaviour for the octopus's actions to this point. What followed, however, lends support to the opinion that octopuses are also intelligent; they can solve a problem and remember the solution or adapt the solution to a new version of the problem in a way that is consistently faster than trial and error.

What happened next is this. Once the octopus had seen and solved the problem of getting the crab out of the jar, the experiment was repeated. In successive trials the octopus no longer attacked the jar in an attempt to capture the crab in its web but moved to the jar, located the cork and pulled the cork out to gain immediate access to the crab. Once the researchers were certain that the octopus had learned and remembered the solution, they introduced another level of complexity by adding a locking pin to the cork so that the pin had to be removed before the cork could be removed.

The octopus's initial response was to try what had worked before. When that did not achieve results, it further explored the cork and—by accident or not—dislodged the locking pin, pulled the cork and seized the crab. In future trials the octopus moved directly to the locking pin and then removed the cork. It had learned and remembered the solution to the problem. To learn from experience is part of the definition of intelligence.

When this information was published in the scientific literature, a number of other researchers were interested in duplicating the experiment to see if they got similar results. Some used the same species of octopus, and others used different species. In most cases similar results were reported, but there were several additional and interesting outcomes. In one case the glass jar was left in the aquarium with the octopus. At the time of the experimental trial the crab was put into the jar and the jar sealed while the octopus watched. The octopus was able to solve the problems, and then it took the solution one step forward. When the researcher approached the aquarium, the octopus left its den and quickly moved into the glass jar to await the arrival of the crab! Is that abstract thought? It certainly could be inter-preted that way.

In an underwater experiment Jim conducted for a French film crew using a large male giant Pacific octopus, he obtained similar results, although the reward was not food but escape from a large plastic box. "We had constructed a large rectangular box of clear plastic. At one end of the box was a hole that we were able to make smaller by inserting other pieces of plastic. The filmmakers wanted to show that a relatively large octopus could escape from the box through a very small hole because the octopus has no bones. While this was interest-ing from the filmmakers' visual perspective, I was more inter-ested in seeing how the giant Pacific octopus would cope with the problem.

"The giant Pacific octopus we used was a good-sized male weighing about 28 kg (60 lb) that could easily reach all sides of the box at once. The plastic box was mounted on a frame to hold it above the bottom so that the oc-topus could be filmed from all angles including from under-neath. We also took the time to ensure the box was level, so that the octopus did not have a clue from gravity as to where the escape hole was. Once the octopus was placed in the box, the plastic lid was closed and secured.

SMARTER THAN YOU THINK?

How smart is the giant Pacific octopus? This is a question that has long interested scientists, and many experiments have been developed to investigate this issue. Studies using mazes, in which food is used as a reward for finding the correct route, demonstrate that the octopus learns from its experience and can remember the solution even when deprived of practice for some time. Experiments also show that the octopus can solve a new maze faster than the initial maze, and one assumes that it has been able to adapt its experience from one maze to another. Some scientists see this as proof of intelligence, while others argue that this merely shows the flexibility of the giant Pacific octopus's innate ability and is not true intelligence.

"In the first trial the octopus spent some time exploring the box. It also pushed and pulled on various portions of the box with a focus on the lid, so it was clear to me that it knew where it had entered. On several occasions the tips of arms discovered the exit hole but moved on to explore more of the box. After a few minutes the octopus appeared satisfied that there was only one escape route and it squeezed out of the exit hole, much to the delight and amazement of the cameraman.

"A short time later the same octopus was returned to the box so that it could be filmed from a different angle. In this trial the octopus spent little time in locating the exit hole and squeezing out. It did not waste any time exploring or testing the box but simply escaped as quickly as it could. That generally took about 60 seconds.

"Of interest were the trials conducted on succeeding days when the octopus had rested overnight. Never again did it waste time exploring or testing the box, but always moved directly to the escape hole. Clearly it had learned and remembered the solution to the problem."

People over 40 may recall visiting old-fashioned zoos where animals were kept in sterile cages with little thought to their emotional or psychological needs. In many cases the animals displayed abnormal behaviours such as continuous pacing or deterioration in health, sometimes to the point of death. In modern zoos a great deal of effort is devoted to providing captive animals with as natural an environment as possible. The desired outcome is the normal behaviour of the captive animals including reproductive success, given that some species exist only in zoos.

Drs. Jennifer Mather and Roland Anderson have also looked at the issue of intelligence in giant Pacific octopuses in an aquarium situation. Octopuses at the Seattle Aquarium were given a series of trials with different toys to see what, if anything, would be of interest to them. The question being tested concerned the enhancement of the environment for the octopus. The results were mixed, as is often the case with this kind of experiment, but there are strong indications that giant Pacific octopuses are aware of their surroundings and will engage in non-traditional activities that do not result in any obvious reward other than the satisfaction of playing.

An aquarium that Jim visited on Roanoke Island in North Carolina conducted experiments to challenge its captive octopuses. In this case different foods were hidden inside an assortment of objects, while other objects did not contain food. In total 24 various objects were presented, some with food and some without, some that floated and some that sat on the bottom. There was also a variety of 13 different foods provided at different times, as the octopuses were fed once per day. In addition to observing what foods and objects were preferred, the general activity of each octopus was observed and recorded three times per day. Heather Bates-White, the aquarist in charge of the octopus enrichment project, supplied data on three different octopuses. One was a Pacific Ocean *Octopus bimaculatus* or *O. bimaculoides*, and the other two were *Octopus vulgaris* from the Atlantic ocean.

As one would expect, the results varied from individual to individual, but there were strong likes and dislikes. For example, the two *O. vulgaris* eagerly devoured clams; the other did not eat them at the beginning but eventually grew to tolerate them, although they were not a favourite. One of the *O. vulgaris* ate frozen sardines, while the other just made a mess of them. Foods that all three would eat every time were frozen shrimp and live fish that the octopuses could hunt and capture.

Their individuality was also revealed in the particular objects they selected. One of the *O. vulgaris* liked a floating watering can if it had food in it, while the other *O. vulgaris* examined the can only once. Clearly each octopus was making choices based on some kind of assessment of the available resources and was selecting some while rejecting others.

One of the higher levels of intelligence is the ability to identify oneself. As humans develop, we reach a point at which we recognize ourselves in a mirror or in photographs. We can identify our voice on a recording. A number of researchers have looked at this issue with cephalopods in several ways. In an experiment Jim conducted for the French film crew, a large polished stainless steel plate functioned well as a mirror. The mirror was placed upright on the bottom where it was anticipated the octopus would walk when released. When the octopus walked by the mirror, the only reaction seen was a very brief startle response to something else moving where previously there was nothing. There was no evidence of recognition, interest or awareness. None of the octopuses stopped or approached or touched the mirror. Jim suspects they did not even recognize the image as another octopus; otherwise they would have reacted. Cannibalism is common in giant Pacific octopuses, and avoiding a potential predator or recognizing a potential food source is important in normal living.

Clearly, if giant Pacific octopuses are intelligent, it is not to the level of self-awareness. But are giant Pacific octopuses, or octopuses in general, intelligent? The debate rages on, and there is no general agreement among scientists today. If you are especially interested in this discussion, read Eugene Linden's 2002 book *The Octopus and the Orangutan*. There you can learn about a number of experiments that have been done and how they are interpreted. Included are the comments of several respected scientists on opposite sides of this issue. There is, however, much more that we as humans need to know before we can be sure we are designing our experiments properly and interpreting the results correctly. We are working with an alien group of animals and cannot expect that they want anything to do with us or our agendas.

A BITING ISSUE

Being bitten by a giant Pacific octopus or even the smaller Pacific red octopus can be a serious matter. A giant Pacific octopus and a Pacific red octopus have a beak and a pair of salivary glands (see Chapter Three). One gland produces toxin, and the other produces a powerful saliva that causes tissue to dissolve. Although a giant Pacific octopus seldom bites, the beak can be as large as an adult parrot's and is powerful enough to chip hard clam shells. It stands to reason that being bitten by a beak this strong is painful and will undoubtedly cause bruising even if the skin is not punctured.

While working at the Alaska SeaLife Center in Seward, aquarist Vallorie Hodges examined behavioural responses of giant Pacific octopuses to feeding and handling. As part of this study, she set up an exhibit with a small male octopus in a touch pool, where she would do brief talks for aquarium visitors. Vallorie

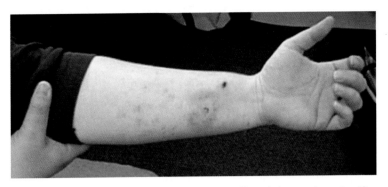

An intern at the Alaska SeaLife Center suffered these giant Pacific octopus bites when she let a small male climb onto her arm. The bites hurt and left bruises, but otherwise had no lasting effects.
Photo Vallorie Hodges, courtesy Alaska SeaLife Center

trained an intern to do the educational talks, but one day things went wrong. "She did fine for quite some time, but finally had an error in judgment and let the animal get more than two arms attached to her arm and lost control of the situation. He bit her twice before she managed to disentangle herself while not skipping a beat of her talk. She later had a little dizziness, nausea and shortness of breath that she thought might have been attributed to her anxiety, being worried she was envenomated." Fortunately the bites healed, and there were no long-term issues.

In other cases where the skin has been punctured, the bites have caused excessive bleeding, and sometimes the wounds have been very slow to heal. This is likely due to saliva being injected into the wound. Both Dr. Anderson and Jim report that the bite of a Pacific red octopus feels more like a sting than a bite (see Chapter Seven).

Scuba divers are seldom bothered by giant Pacific octopuses, but occasionally very aggressive behaviours have been reported. These are likely the result of the fact that the octopuses are "eating machines" in the prime of their lives, putting on about one percent of their body weight per day. Everything they encounter is potentially a meal and is checked out thoroughly with the chemotactic suckers. Several scientific papers, including a recent publication by Dr. Anderson, Jim and others, document giant Pacific octopus "attacks" on divers.

Close Encounters

T he giant Pacific octopus exhibits an amazing repertoire of behaviours, many of which defy simple explanations. We asked several naturalists, aquarists and photographers to share their experiences.

LOUSY NEIGHBOURS

Danny Kent is the curator of BC Waters at the Vancouver Aquarium Marine Science Centre in Stanley Park. Danny has been diving for more than two decades and has worked at the Vancouver Aquarium for the past 20 years. In his experience with giant Pacific octopuses, he has learned that they are highly individual animals that seem to be curious when interacting with divers. He is fascinated by the fluidity of octopuses and their ability to fit through the smallest openings.

When exhibiting octopuses, Danny noted, "Octopus displays sometimes get criticized as being too small, but in my experience they are den-dwelling

Opposite: A giant Pacific octopus captivates Jacqueline Bagan at the Vancouver Aquarium. Octopuses are not the most lively display animals, since they are reclusive and often remain hidden in their dens, venturing out only to feed. Photo Noel Hendrickson

As curator of BC Waters at the Vancouver Aquarium, Danny Kent has had the rare opportunity to dive in Canada's Arctic waters, collecting marine life for display.
Photo Philip Bruecker

animals that are more at home in an exhibit where they can hide in a cave or squeeze into a crevice out of view. Historically I think the aquarium used to collect relatively large giant Pacific octopuses that were impressive display animals, but in the past decade or so we have tried to take a different approach. We figured that by collecting the larger giant Pacific octopuses we were removing potentially reproductive adults from the wild. They were already near the end of their lifespan and wouldn't be around for long. Now we try to collect them as juveniles and raise them in reserve tanks behind the scenes. This way we can monitor their growth over time and get them accustomed to being handled and fed by an aquarist. Stimpy was a four-gram (0.14 oz) octopus that we collected in December 1997 that lived at the Vancouver Aquarium until June 2000, when it finally died weighing 29.6 kg (65.3 lb). When it died, its total body length [tip of mantle to tip of longest arm] was 196 cm (77 in) and its largest sucker diameter was 8.9 cm (3.5 in)."

Giant Pacific octopuses on display sometimes make lousy neighbours. Danny observed, "We have seen them eat dogfish, skates, rockfish and herring, as some examples of their tank mates. The list is likely longer, but we don't always see it! Each giant Pacific octopus is different, however, and some individuals can live with schools of rockfish for years and not eat them, while others rapidly pick off all of their tank mates in no time. Another giant Pacific octopus that lived in our large 300,000 l (65,000 gal) Strait of Georgia exhibit liked to crawl up the side of the rockwork near the water surface and then sit with one arm extended into the water column, waiting for a herring to swim by and bump into the arm. Kind of like the octopus version of fishing, using its arm as the rod!"

Danny finds that octopuses differ widely in their personalities. "Some are definitely more shy, and others are more interactive with the aquarists. Some will climb right out of the exhibit to take food from the aquarist's hand. Some like to come up to the surface and crawl all over the aquarist's hands and arms. I guess they are just checking them out from a tactile and chemical sensing perspective."

THE BEST PHOTOGRAPH NEVER TAKEN

Naturalist and author Andy Lamb first started working at the Vancouver Aquarium in 1966 as an aquarist and chief collector, later as a school program coordinator. As a veteran diver certified in 1967, he has encountered many giant Pacific octopuses during his explorations along the West Coast and at the aquarium.

Andy remembers one particular giant Pacific octopus that lived in a reserve tank next to a garburator. "It got to know when the aquarists would visit the garburator (likely by the sound or vibration of the metal grates in the floor) and would shoot water (via its siphon) out the top of the tank—this usually resulted in any unsuspecting person getting doused with a shower of freezing salt water. While the octopus had obviously learned to perform this trick, we regular staffers also learned to tread lightly to avoid a soaking."

Certified as a diver in 1967, naturalist Andy Lamb worked for many years as an aquarist and chief collector at the Vancouver Aquarium, and has had many memorable encounters with octopuses.
Photo Peter Luckham

While Andy was busy working with Bernie Hanby on their 2005 book *Marine Life of the Pacific Northwest,* he had a memorable encounter. He recalled, "Each summer I used to visit my friend Charlie Moffet at Brown Island in the San Juan Islands. This time Bernie and I were diving on the west side of San Juan Island from Charlie's boat. We were having a good dive, finding numerous creatures to photograph as well as enjoying good visibility. About halfway through the dive, we found a seven-kilogram (15 lb) giant Pacific octopus in a rocky den. This individual was in the mood to play and began emerging from its shelter. At this point Bernie noticed that he was out of film. 'Damn'—or other expletives—could be heard in muffled form. I signalled to Bernie to head to the boat, get his second camera and return, while I waited with our newly found friend. So off he went. Meanwhile the octopus continued to befriend me. Initially it slowly crawled out and began to climb on my head. Ultimately this amazing octopus completely covered my mask. Everything went black. Then it began to tug on my mask (which flooded) and my regulator. At this point I decided that it was time to persuade my eight-armed buddy to reverse this process. Fortunately, with some gentle arm twisting, it retreated slowly. Eventually I was able to clear my mask and watch the friendly creature move down my arm. The entire interaction seemed to last many minutes but likely was much shorter. Just about the time that the octopus was disappearing into its den, Bernie (armed with his second camera and a fresh roll of film) arrived, ready to shoot. Another 'Damn!' No doubt the result is some of the best octopus-diver photographs never taken."

Andy also had an unforgettable experience with a golf-ball-sized ruby octopus. "While teaching an intertidal marine biology program at the aquarium, I was demonstrating the biology of molluscs with some live animals. The star of this presentation was an adult ruby octopus. I let the little fellow crawl about on my hand while the students gently touched it. At this point the creature decided to bite me with its tiny but powerful beak. It hurt! But not wanting to spoil the moment and make the students uncomfortable, I carried on with the demonstration and educational patter. Eventually a considerable amount of blood became visible, and word spread throughout the class. By the end of the session, the bleeding had stopped, although a fair amount of pain remained. Over the next few hours my hand swelled considerably. Although the pain disappeared that night, the swelling remained for about ten days. No lasting damage occurred."

A LIFE-LONG FASCINATION

Dr. Roland Anderson has worked at the Seattle Aquarium on the Puget Sound waterfront for over 30 years. Inspired by his older brother, who was in the US Navy diving program, he started diving in 1966 and was soon hooked by the beautiful marine life he saw. He became fascinated by giant Pacific octopuses early in his career and has published nearly 50 papers about cephalopods. He oversees an annual Puget Sound octopus survey by divers every spring in which volunteer divers search out the animals and report back with numbers and sizes of giant Pacific octopuses discovered.

Aquarist and cephalopod researcher Roland Anderson observes Mr. Big at the Seattle Aquarium. Mr. Big weighed 43 kg (95 lb) when he finally died of old age. Photo Leo Shaw, Seattle Aquarium

Over his many years as a biologist, Roland has had some notorious characters in the Seattle Aquarium tanks. "We had one giant Pacific octopus we named Emily Dickenson [a notoriously shy poet] that hid behind the fibreglass backdrop at the back of the tank and didn't want to be seen by the public. Another called Leisure Suit Larry [a video game character] would have been cited for sexual harassment if he were a human, because his arms were all over you. Each night, Lucretia McEvil tore up her tank, biting through the nylon cable ties that held the under-gravel filter together, leaving me to fix everything in the morning.

"Another octopus regularly squirted a night biologist as she passed by the tank. Only her. Turns out she would shine her bright light on the tank to check water flow and disturb it from its nighttime reveries. I have recently been studying if octopuses can recognize individual people, which has been stated anecdotally in various articles. I believe that they can, and Dr. Jennifer Mather and I are writing up the paper now."

Roland reported that the largest giant Pacific octopuses displayed at the Seattle Aquarium were close to 45 kg (100 lb). "Mr. Big was 43 kg (95 lb). Another that was removed from our dome tank after passing away of old age weighed 44 kg (97 lb). The biggest specimen that I know of collected by a diver from Puget Sound was 53 kg (117 lb)."

Even after his many years of experience, giant Pacific octopuses still fascinate Roland. He continues his research into their behaviour; studying senescence (the process of growing old), experimenting with enrichment in aquariums and trying to determine just how smart they really are. On that last note, he and Dr. Mather have observed octopuses engaging in play behaviour, using tools, employing landmark navigation and displaying various personality traits. All of these suggest a creature with remarkable intelligence for an invertebrate. It's nearly impossible to state exactly how smart they are, but Roland put it this way: "I believe they are smarter than fish, amphibians, reptiles and most birds. Not as smart as parrots. Maybe as smart as a crow."

MEETING THE BEAST

Biologist and author Jim Cosgrove had an unanticipated encounter with a giant Pacific octopus while working at the Undersea Gardens, then located in Oak Bay, near Victoria. The Pacific Undersea Gardens is a floating aquarium where guests descend stairs into a submerged theatre with viewing windows about 3.5 m (11 ft) below sea level. People sit on bleachers to watch scheduled shows. Jim recalled, "As a display diver it was my job to bring various animals up close to the windows while a guide described them to the spectators. The culmination of the 20-minute show was for me to bring out an octopus, which never failed to thrill the crowd.

"There were a number of fibreglass 'rocks' bolted to the bottom. These rocks looked real to the audience, but they were actually hollow at the back. They were a good place for an octopus to hide, and it was relatively easy to get an octopus out for the show.

The Pacific Undersea Gardens in Victoria's Inner Harbour gives visitors a unique opportunity to descend below sea level to view captive marine life.
Photo Jim Cosgrove

"One day as I entered the water, I checked a den immediately under the entry ladder and saw that there were not one but two octopuses inside. I thought that was very unusual, but I didn't have time to look any further and carried on with the show. Then came time for the octopus to star, and off I went. I started rousting the octopus out of the den and could see that the second octopus was starting to move as well. Darn, I thought, I'm going to have two of them out at the same time, which will spoil the show since at least half the people will be watching the one wandering around.

"At that point I noticed that the arms slithering by my mask were getting larger and larger with the biggest suckers I had ever seen. Then I realized that this was, in fact, not two octopuses but just one monster. By this time I was seized by the octopus, and all I could do was keep both hands on my regulator while the octopus dragged me around like a sack of potatoes. At one point I was able to see that the octopus could reach from the display windows to the outside screen, which was a distance of 6.7 m (22 ft), so this octopus had a radial span of just over this distance.

"After a short time—it seemed like several lifetimes to me—the octopus let me go and I beat a hasty retreat to the dive ladder. I emerged to hoots of laughter from the other divers who had known that the beast was in there but deliberately neglected to tell me.

"No one ever bothered that animal again, but it did not live more than a few weeks. When it died, we took it over to the Oak Bay Marina, where it was put on the scales. Its wet weight was 71 kg (156 lb), and that remains the largest octopus I have ever had personal contact with."

Jim has a lifetime supply of octopus stories. "Two divers—one who wishes to remain unidentified and is willing to pay me to do so—were in the Mediterranean when one of them discovered a small octopus. Thinking to pull a joke on his partner, the diver picked up the octopus, took off his mask, put the octopus inside and then slipped his mask back on, clearing out the water. He then swam over to get his partner's attention. The octopus, meanwhile, was not thrilled with this whole process and being high and dry, began to look for a convenient place to hide. The human face has few hiding places but the octopus began to explore by running an arm inside the diver's nose! Needless to say the mask came off in a hurry and the octopus was free to go on its way. The other diver almost choked to death with laughter.

"My wife Jeannie and I were diving one day when we passed by a small pinnacle of rock about a metre (3 ft) high. Perched on top of this pinnacle was a small giant Pacific octopus that was doing its best to look like the rock. We slowly approached it and were able to move quite close before it became frightened. We stayed our distance, and after a few minutes the octopus appeared to be satisfied that we were not a threat. It changed colour and slowly raised itself on the rock to look at us more carefully. After several minutes of watching us, it cautiously reached out with one of the front arms and started to feel my suit. Jeannie backed off a bit to watch this, and I allowed the octopus to explore. After a few moments the octopus crawled over onto me and crawled up and over my head and then down my back. Jeannie was able to watch as it explored my tank and then crawled back over me and onto its rock again. It just sat there flashing colours as we moved off.

"A long-time friend, Jim Mendria, and I were doing a photo dive north of Port Hardy on Vancouver Island. We had just finished videotaping a beautiful juvenile wolf-eel when we noticed a small giant Pacific octopus coming up a cliff face. I positioned myself to lie flat on the bottom with the video camera recording. The octopus came over the edge of the cliff and stopped when it first saw me. Then, gripping the rocks with it rear legs, it slowly stretched out its front pair of arms to touch the arms of my lighting system. Through the viewfinder I could see the back arms quickly release and reattach to the bottom as the octopus slowly crept forward, and more of its arms covered my head and the camera. Eventually my head and shoulders were completely engulfed in the octopus's web, and all I could see through the viewfinder were the small suckers surrounding the mouth and the mouth itself. Then the octopus decided to see if it could figure out what I was and started to pull on my suit and the camera lights, so I decided to lift off the bottom. Startled at having the bottom move, the octopus released me and jetted off.

"Several years ago at the Ogden Point breakwater, I had taken my camera along on a dive to photograph some of the marine life. At one point we discovered an octopus midden and stopped to see if there was an octopus in the den. I settled on to the bottom and flattened out so that I could peer into the den. Within seconds I felt myself slide down the rocks and I thought this strange, as the slope was not that steep. I tried to dig the tips of my fins into the rocks for purchase, only to discover that my fins and lower legs had been seized by a small giant Pacific octopus. It was pulling me down the slope toward its den. I was able to push myself upright, and once the octopus saw the size of what it had captured, it let go and beat a hasty retreat. Unknowingly I had flopped my fins almost over the entrance to a lower den that I had not noticed when we arrived.

"For many years I had searched for a nesting female octopus but I had never found one. Even in areas where I dived every week and knew every major den, I had never found a nesting female. One day I was working for a film crew doing a shoot for Mutual of Omaha's *Wild Kingdom*. We were in Saanich Inlet, and my job was to locate an octopus that I could capture and tag for the film crew. My partner and I swam a very familiar route, checking known den sites as we went. At one of the deeper dens we noticed that the entrance was filled in with rocks and there was only a very old midden. Nevertheless, we were getting concerned about not finding an octopus for filming, so I moved some of the rocks and shone my light inside. To my complete surprise and delight, I was looking at a female giant Pacific octopus and a full nest of eggs! We returned to the boat and informed the film crew of this incredible find and how lucky they were. Imagine my disappointment when I was told that this was not part of what they wanted to film and they did not want to waste a dive on it. We did eventually find an octopus for them to film, but it was bittersweet to have discovered my first nesting female octopus and then be told that it wasn't in the script.

"On another occasion I was working with a German film crew in Saanich Inlet, and they had just arrived in Victoria that morning. A bit jetlagged, they did not want to do a full day on the water, so as part of a familiarization dive I had taken the cameraman down so that he could see what the bottom and visibility were like. He took the camera just to test for leaks and check all functions. As luck would have it we found an octopus at about 12 m (40 ft) out in the open, a rare event. I moved over, picked up the octopus and held it for the cameraman. To my surprise the octopus jetted straight up and just kept going! In about four breaths it had reached the surface, much to the surprise of the rest of the camera crew and my partner. I had never had a giant Pacific octopus do this before, and I thought this was a great start to the shoot, a unique piece of footage! Unfortunately the cameraman had decided this was not something he was interested in and did not get the shot. Little did he know what he had missed!"

THE STAR OF REALITY TV

In 1994, while filming an episode of the popular TV series *Sport Diver*, naturalist and photographer Doug Pemberton and the show's producer Danny Mauro had a giant Pacific octopus encounter that almost made them famous. As Doug recalled, "We had headed out aboard the dive boat *Nautilus* for four days of filming in Sechelt Inlet, north of Vancouver. One of the dive sites was just outside Tzoonie Narrows, where at 21 m (70 ft) I spotted crab carapaces and remains that indicated there might be an octopus under the nearby rock. Just as I dropped lower to have a look with my hand light, I landed directly on top of another octopus that was so well camouflaged I hadn't even seen it. It immediately jetted off with Danny in hot pursuit with his video camera.

"I stayed at the rock and dropped closer to the bottom so that I could have a good look inside. Sure enough, there was an octopus at home. I had my hands close to the entrance to the den and before long a single arm tip emerged and felt my left hand. Then a second arm came out and felt around my other hand. A second later, the whole octopus seemed to explode from the den, enveloping my head. I've encountered plenty of octopuses before and wasn't too concerned, but you don't want to let an octopus get a good grip on your mask or regulator, because that could become

In this image captured from videotape, Doug Pemberton gets a faceful of belligerent giant Pacific octopus. There's a significant chance of having a mask flooded or a regulator pulled out, so the authors urge inexperienced divers not to let an octopus touch them. Photo Danny Mauro

a big problem. And this one seemed determined to do just that. So I started to pull at its arms to prevent losing my scuba mouthpiece."

In the meantime, Danny had seen the commotion and started to film the encounter, which he knew would make for entertaining television. He was having some trouble adjusting his buoyancy because he was fairly new to drysuit diving, but he managed to record most of Doug's mini-battle. Doug finally managed to extricate himself from the attention of the overly curious octopus and they continued their dive.

Little did Doug and Danny know what kind of media monster they had created.

After that episode of *Sport Diver* was released, Danny started getting phone calls out of the blue from reality TV shows that wanted to use the footage. Other shows took it even further, shooting recreations of the event. During the making of *When*

Fun Turns To Fear, a limp white piece of fish-shop octopus was draped over Doug's mask in order to get the close-ups they needed. It looked so ridiculous that Doug and cameraman McDaniel nearly drowned, they laughed so hard. But that was only the beginning. This monster was taking on a life of its own.

Next came calls from producers with the Oprah Winfrey, Montel Williams and Sally Jessie Raphael shows, wanting to fly Doug all over North America to tell rapt studio audiences how he was nearly devoured by a giant killer octopus. When Doug calmly explained that he was never in any real danger and that it was no big deal, they promptly said goodbye and hung up.

The video footage made its inevitable way onto YouTube, and millions around the world got to see Doug "attacked." That generated even more interest from sensationalized reality shows. Doug notes that the only program that treated the encounter with any sort of truthfulness was produced by the New Zealand Natural History Unit.

So why did a giant Pacific octopus leave the cold comforts of its den to climb all over Doug's head? There's no pat answer to that question. Octopuses are complex creatures and exhibit behaviours that often defy any reasonable explanation. Maybe Doug looked like dinner. Or perhaps the octopus was just seeking a little face time on YouTube.

A STRANGE ENCOUNTER

Randy Haight, a Vancouver Island videographer who has filmed cephalopods around the world, had his first octopus encounter in a dive shop in Australia in February 1983. "A diver returning rental gear pulled a snail shell out of his buoyancy compensator pocket, and a small creature fell out and plopped on the floor. As I went to pick it up someone yelled, "Don't touch it!" The shop owner came running over with a spatula, scooped it up and put the blue-ringed octopus into his saltwater aquarium. He then explained that this golf-ball-sized animal could have killed me with one toxin-laden bite. This scary revelation fascinated me and from that point on I was completely hooked on octopuses.

"Over the years I spent much of my time seeking out octopuses to learn more about them. At Saltery Bay, near my former home in Powell River, I had an unusual relationship with a 1.5 m (5 ft) male giant Pacific octopus. I used to take an oyster from shore and deliver it opened outside the den. After about six dives the octopus would emerge as I arrived, and we would interact briefly before it retreated with the snack. I gave the oyster to other divers and stayed out of sight, but it wouldn't come out unless it could see me from the den.

"Another three-metre (10 ft) male I visited on Texada Island displayed similar tendencies and really seemed to enjoy human interaction. I took divers there regularly to have an octopus

In this image captured from videotape, a large male giant Pacific octopus faces into the current and spreads his arms so the suckers can taste the water for the presence of a female. Note the amputated first right arm and some missing arm tips. Whether these battle wounds are from rival males or from predators is unknown. Photo Randy Haight

experience. It would sit on my arm for several minutes while divers felt its arms and took pictures.

"In September 1992, while on a film shoot at Quadra Island, BC, I noticed a large octopus above us atop a rock outcrop. I watched it rear up and orient itself into the slight current. I tried to signal the rest of the crew, but as I was doing the underwater lighting, I had to concentrate on my task. That peculiar behaviour seemed bizarre, almost surreal. I told the other divers about it, but I think they thought I was exaggerating.

"In January 1998 my friend Hans Schmid and I were finishing off the last of his open-water dives in Powell River. Visibility was glorious, up to 30 m (98 ft). When we arrived at a popular octopus dive site, a male octopus I was familiar with was sitting just outside his den. I noticed he had lost parts of a couple more arms since I had last visited him. Both Hans and I touched him briefly, then he shuffled off toward the largest rock on the featureless sand bottom. As it started up the rock, I got into a good position to shoot video. When he started to rear up, I got so excited I could hardly contain myself.

"The octopus oriented itself into the slight current and reared up into the water column. After the second time it reared up, Hans handled it briefly then released it. It went right back up on the rock and did it again. Several times it reached out and gently grasped the lens of my underwater housing and my drysuit. At one point I pulled off my glove to let him have a really good smell-taste of me. After about 40 minutes with this magnificent creature, I picked him up and carried him the short distance back to his den, and he slithered inside.

"I don't know if Hans ever understood why I was so excited after getting out of the water, but of the hundreds of dives with octopuses I have done, this was perhaps the most extraordinary."

TEN FRIGID MINUTES

Scuba instructor extraordinaire Jim Willoughby taught thousands to dive in BC and eventually retired near Powell River. He has had plenty of photographic encounters with octopuses, but one in particular stands out. As Jim recalled, "I once received a call

A teeny-weeny green bikini is not really suitable attire for an encounter with a monster giant Pacific octopus in bone-chilling water. But that's what the *National Enquirer* wanted, so Miriam March bravely persevered for photographer Jim Willoughby.
Photo Jim Willoughby

from *National Enquirer* about using one of my giant Pacific octopus photos. Just so that you don't get it confused with *National Geographic*, the *National Enquirer* is the one found at grocery-store checkouts. They wanted a photo of a lady diver holding an octopus, so I agreed to send them several slides, providing they promised not to make the octopus out as a slimy denizen of the deep that sinks ships and eats the crews.

"In about a week I received another call, complaining that the girl in the photos was wearing a wetsuit. They informed me that she must be wearing a bikini. After collecting myself, I calmly advised them of the water temperature in BC. In a few words, it's very cold! That didn't seem to bother them, as they still wanted to know if I could meet their request. When I hung up the phone, I wondered which insane asylum to check into.

"After an extensive search, I finally found a gutsy young lady named Miriam March willing to do this. I had previously done some underwater photography at the Undersea Gardens in Victoria Harbour and explained the situation to them. The curator thought it would be great publicity and readily agreed to host us. The Undersea Gardens is a building that floats in the harbour with the underwater viewing areas enclosed—it is much like an aquarium but is actually part of the ocean.

"As my diving buddy David March and I submerged, the sight was breathtaking. We were in an enclosed area about four metres (12 ft) deep containing colourful rockfishes, anemones, wolf-eels and much more. But our mission was not about any of these creatures—we were looking for the elusive giant Pacific octopus. David's job was to find the octopus and bring it to Miriam, our bikini-clad model. My job was to take as many pictures as I could of her holding it for the short time she could endure the frigid water.

"It was a cold, bleak November day, and a brisk wind blew rain in sheets across Victoria Harbour. Miriam waited patiently, clad only in a tiny green bikini and her diving gear. She was covered with a huge blanket to keep her warm. When I gave her the signal, she jumped in with grim determination and sheer guts, knowing she was about to accomplish something no one had ever attempted.

"David handed her the octopus. The next few minutes were filled with clouds of ink, sucker discs, excitement and an occasional glimpse of Miriam, who almost lost her tank once and her mask twice. Amid this chaos it was my job to frame this thrashing mass of arms and Miriam and fire the shutter. After an amazing 10 minutes immersed in the icy waters wrestling with this huge creature, Miriam had finally had enough!

"From the cold waters of the Undersea Gardens emerged a tired, shaken but very brave lady. She had probably set a record—10 minutes in the frigid water with only a green bikini and a giant octopus to keep her warm. The *National Enquirer* was very excited about the pictures. But their readers would never know how difficult it is to get an underwater photo of a girl in a bikini holding a giant Pacific octopus!"

Fisheries

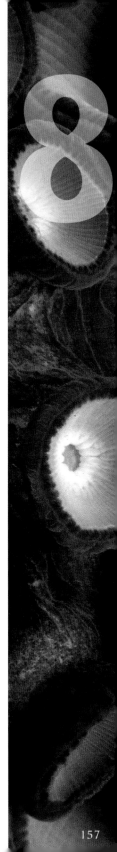

Octopuses, squids and cuttlefishes are a major source of protein for human consumption worldwide. Today it is estimated that fishers take more than 3 million tonnes (3.3 million tons) worth more than six billion dollars annually. Along the Pacific coast of North America, giant Pacific octopuses have been captured for food and used as bait for hundreds of years.

First Nations people have a long history of hunting devilfish (octopuses) at low tide and in shallow water by looking for large rocks with clam and crab shell heaps nearby. Some hunters used a simple sharply pointed stick, repeatedly stabbing the octopus until it came out of the den or grabbed the spear. Others used a hooked stick to probe the inside of the den; if the stick was grabbed, the hunter would stab and gradually pull the octopus out. Some hunters used a pointed, barbed stick pushed into the octopus and exerted a steady pull until the octopus released its hold. These tools are found in many museum collections, including the Royal BC Museum in Victoria. Octopuses were an important food source and were also favoured as bait for halibut fishing. Pieces were cut and frayed, then tied onto a hook.

BRAINY ARMS

More than half of an octopus's neurons are in its arms. Experiments have shown that severed arms will continue to slither about for some time as if they were still attached. Captured animals eviscerated by commercial dive harvesters continue to crawl about in a seemingly normal fashion for several minutes.

Octopus flesh also had medicinal uses. According to David Ellis and Luke Swan in *Teachings of the Tides*, the Haida of the Queen Charlotte Islands used the legs of octopuses to bandage burns. A fresh, unskinned leg was wrapped around a burn and tied tightly. New skin was said to form quickly over the burn because the octopus leg prevented air from reaching the skin.

FISHERIES PAST AND PRESENT

Sandy Matheson, a veteran commercial fisher, told of his early days in the late 1960s when he hunted giant Pacific octopuses in Discovery Passage near Campbell River during the winter months. Sandy used to fish from a small skiff powered by a Briggs & Stratton inboard engine, cruising slowly along the shoreline on calm days when he could see far down into the clear, cold water. Standing in the bow with a rope around his waist to steer the boat, he would use a six-metre (20 ft) gaff to hook octopuses that he spotted. In those days he got 10 cents a pound and usually managed to catch 90 kg (200 lb) a day, which put $20 in his pocket. The halibut fishers would skin and freeze the octopuses for use as bait.

Commercial fisheries today include trap and dive fisheries as well as a limited bycatch trawl fishery. In BC most of the dive

Opposite: Mike Richmond of Campbell River, who used to capture giant Pacific octopuses commercially for halibut bait, displays a day's catch in Discovery Passage. Photo Fred Bavendam

fisheries occur on the east and south coasts of Vancouver Island, from Port Hardy at the north end to Sooke far south on Juan de Fuca Strait. The reported annual landings of octopus have fluctuated widely. They averaged less than 22 tonnes (24 tons) until 1987, then increased to 200 tonnes (220 tons) in the late 1980s when demand for halibut bait increased. The fishery reached a peak at 217 tonnes (239 tons)—118 tonnes (130 tons) from the dive fishery and 99 tonnes (109 tons) from the trap and trawl fishery—in 1997, but landings have decreased to 26 tonnes (28.7 tons) in 2005. Demand for octopus as bait declined when halibut quotas assigned on an individual basis made the fishery less competitive.

Fishers, especially those in the halibut fleet, favour the use of octopus meat because its firm, rubbery texture makes it last a long time on their longline hooks. The market for food-quality octopus is limited but seems to be expanding, with both European and Asian buyers distributing the meat.

Mike Richmond surfaces with a giant Pacific octopus from the waters of Discovery Passage near Campbell River on Vancouver Island.
Photo Fred Bavendam

Octopuses seek out confined spaces as dens, and this makes it possible to capture them in specially constructed traps. Deployed in suitable areas, the traps are pulled to the surface at regular intervals to remove the unsuspecting animals that have moved into the convenient homes.

In the late 1970s Dr. Brian Hartwick, a marine biologist at Simon Fraser University funded by the Department of Fisheries and Oceans, carried out extensive studies of various trap types off Tofino on the west coast of Vancouver Island. His research confirmed that traditional cedar box traps similar to those used in Washington and Oregon were superior to tire traps or plastic tubes. He also found that offshore catches in water up to 110 m (360 ft) deep were three times higher (13 percent capture efficiency) than inshore catches (4 percent). Octopus catch rates were low in proportion to the fishing costs, and efforts to develop a directed trap fishery were not successful.

OCTOPUS HARVESTERS

On any list of offbeat occupations, octopus harvester has to rank among the strangest. But for Brady Bell, a 48-year-old Vancouver Island man, it seems perfectly natural.

Brady is one of BC's handful of commercial octopus divers, practising a form of harvesting that began around 1979. An underwater harvester for more than 24 years, he estimates that he's made 20,000 scuba dives, give or take a few. It's not a job for the out-of-shape or faint of heart. Brady and his partner must don thick neoprene drysuits to survive the frigid water and strap on a heavy weight belt and scuba tank before venturing down as far as 30 m (98 ft) in search of these secretive cephalopods.

Octopus harvesting is markedly different from harvesting other seafood such as sea cucumbers, scallops or urchins. Octopuses don't simply lie around out in the open waiting to be collected. Instead they hunker down deep in the recesses of rocky caves, presenting a harvester with no end of challenges.

Brady's first task is to locate an area where there is suitable habitat. This usually means a bottom with lots of big boulders or crevices where the animals can make their dens. Once he locates

an octopus, he still faces the considerable problem of getting it out, and this is where controversy surrounds the fishery. Not all octopuses are successfully caught, and the Canadian government does not permit the use of gaffs or spears, which injure too many animals that are not caught. The most effective means of flushing an octopus out of its den is to pump in a chemical irritant. In the past harvesters have used nasty chemicals such as copper sulphate, ammonia and liquid bleach, but these are extremely toxic and kill other marine life within the den and nearby. The federal Department of Fisheries and Oceans no longer permits use of these chemicals, and at present hydrogen peroxide is one of the few effective and approved irritants. Other imaginative methods such as electricity, an octoprod (a handheld rod that delivers an electric jolt) and hot water have been tried with little success.

Brady always makes sure there are no eggs in the den, as he doesn't want to disturb a brooding female. Nor does he take small animals less than seven kilograms (15 lb). Once Brady flushes an octopus from its den, he wrestles it into a mesh bag and eventually takes his catch to the surface. There he kills and eviscerates the animal, stores it in a clear plastic bag and later flash-freezes it.

Generally Brady visits a series of dens at various sites where he knows each rock. He works from a small open skiff, often with his wife Betty and diving partner Pete Brown. "It's like I'm a trapper. I go to the dens, then I come back to them." He usually waits about six weeks before returning to the same place to give migrating octopuses a chance to reoccupy the dens.

The average octopus that Brady catches is 14 to 18 kg (30 to 40 lb), and he lands 136 kg (300 lb) on a decent day. His best single-day catch ever was 544 kg (1,200 lb), a total of 42 octopuses. His market consists primarily of commercial fishers who use the meat for bait, although the food market is improving. In the early 1990s prices were low, but the price has increased over the years to around $1.15 per kg ($2.50 per lb) in 2007.

The fishery is now managed by issuing scientific permits only to experienced harvesters who meet specific criteria. Harvesters are required to collect biological data on each dive, including location, dive time, depth, number of octopuses captured, catch weight and number of brooding females. Fisheries and Oceans Canada compiles this information to enable proper assessment and management of the fishery.

• •

Opposite: Commercial fisher Brady Bell (in the drysuit) prepares for a dive with his partner Pete Brown. The largest giant Pacific octopus he ever harvested in his approximately 20,000 dives weighed about 57 kg (125 lb). Photo Neil McDaniel

Below: Brady's octopus catch is gutted, bagged and frozen for sale as halibut bait. Photo Neil McDaniel

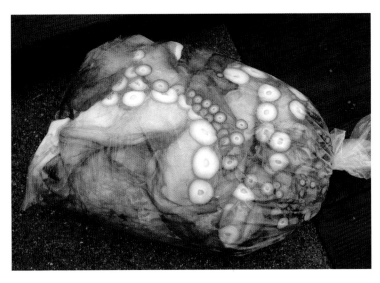

The largest octopus Brady ever caught was taken in Becher Bay on southern Vancouver Island. It weighed 57 kg (125 lb), far larger than his second largest octopus, which was 41 kg (90 lb). He believes that the largest animals are found farther south on Vancouver Island, especially in Juan de Fuca Strait.

Over the years Brady has made some remarkable observations. Once he found a giant Pacific octopus eating a bird, and he has seen sunflower sea stars eating octopus carcasses many times. Although he has handled thousands of octopuses, he has never been bitten.

Cliff Law of Victoria, another experienced octopus harvester, has spent thousands of hours underwater off Vancouver Island. Fishing success fluctuates from year to year; Cliff harvests anywhere from 16,000 to 45,000 kg (35,000 to 100,000 lb) per year. Of his catch 90 percent goes for food, with good markets in Spain and Greece.

The biggest octopus Cliff ever saw, caught by John and Frank McGuire of Victoria, was the monster that mugged Jim at the Undersea Gardens. Over his many years of diving Cliff has seen strange things. Once he found a large octopus that had apparently captured and drowned a sea otter and was busy eating the head. He has also observed octopuses eating mink and diving ducks.

BYCATCH IN PRAWN FISHERIES

Prawn fishing is a profitable deep-water fishery in BC. Interconnected conical mesh traps (50 per string), deployed at depths of 90 to 150 m (295 to 490 ft), are usually baited with dogfish meat. The traps are designed so that two-spot prawns are attracted by the scent of the bait, crawl up an inverted funnel—like the sleeve of a shirt—and get trapped inside.

Octopuses are quite often captured as incidental catch after they are drawn to the crustacean smorgasbord. Generally the bycatch is relatively small, perhaps one or two octopuses in a set of 50 traps, depending upon the depth, type of bottom and season. But once in a while truly incredible numbers show up. Randy Haight, who used to fish prawns commercially in the Powell River area, experienced such an occasion in the late 1990s, when he pulled up 150 traps and found over 400 octopuses—some traps had four or five small animals of one to two kilograms (2.2 to 4.4 lb), with the biggest about 15 kg (33 lb). It's likely that many of the smaller animals were Pacific red octopuses. After a while he lost count—the decks were awash in flailing arms.

Prawn fishers are allowed to keep this octopus bycatch, and most of them freeze and sell it for halibut bait.

OCTOPUS WRESTLING

The rather strange sport of octopus wrestling had its beginnings in Washington state. Using only snorkelling gear, teams of divers had to repeatedly dive, locate octopuses and try to bring the most animals to the surface, where they were weighed. The activity became quite popular and was even televised with up to 5,000 spectators on hand. Afterward the octopuses were eaten, given to a local aquarium or returned to the sea. In April 1963, more than 100 divers took part and captured a total of 25 giant Pacific octopuses, the largest weighing 26 kg (57 lb).

Bill High, a long-time Washington diver and scuba instructor, recalls the early days. "The Puget Sound Mudsharks began the World Octopus Wrestling Championship in either 1955 or 1956. When I joined the club in 1957, the competition was well established. I think the last event was held around 1968. My three-man team took first place in 1961, third place in 1965 and fourth place in 1964. Information about octopuses appeared in *Skin Diver* magazines from the late 1950s and into the 1960s. My research on the giant Pacific octopus was featured in the December 1971 issue of *National Geographic* magazine. In the first years the competition was breath-hold only, but by 1960 there was a scuba component. Most of the annual competitions were held at Titlow Beach in Tacoma, Washington."

On Vancouver Island near Victoria, the octopus wrestling event was called the Octopus Grapple, but the goal was the same: catch as many giant Pacific octopuses as possible and bring them to the surface. Awards went to the team with the greatest weight caught, and an individual award was issued for the largest giant Pacific octopus of all.

1963 World Octopus Wrestling Championships

Seattle divers Dick Peter
Keffler, and Dale Dean
largest octopus capture
the meet—a 57-pound be
Intelligencer photo by To

The host dive club would spend a week or two capturing as many octopuses as they could find and putting them into a cove or bay with suitable habitat. The weekend of the Octopus Grapple would sometimes see more than 100 divers gather in their wetsuits. There were two levels of competition, snorkel and scuba. In the first competition the pairs of snorkellers would head out into the cove and take turns diving to locate an octopus den. Once they located a den, one snorkeller would introduce blue-stone (a solution of copper sulfate, a toxic chemical) into the den. The snorkellers would then alternately watch the den until the octopus came out, when they could capture it and take it to the surface. The scuba portion of the grapple would follow after an hour of the snorkel event.

Fisheries and Oceans Canada eventually banned the use of copper sulfate for flushing octopuses, and octopus grapples have become a thing of the past. Since the banning of copper sulfate, a number of other chemicals have been used to flush octopuses with differing levels of success. Commercial harvesters are now restricted to using only certain irritants to avoid harming other animals in or near the dens.

Top: Octopus-hunting snorkellers venture into the ocean at Saxe Point near Victoria, the site of many octopus grapples held in the 1950s and 1960s. This event was Jim's first introduction to giant Pacific octopuses and inspired him to study these interesting creatures. Photo Jim Cosgrove

Bottom: Octopuses captured during the grapple were brought to shore and displayed in saltwater aquaria, much to the delight of the public. Photo Jim Cosgrove

Opposite: A 1963 issue of *Skin Diver* magazine portrays octopus wrestling as a newsworthy annual event. Eventually this contest was discontinued as a more ecologically sensitive approach to the underwater world developed. Courtesy *Skin Diver* magazine

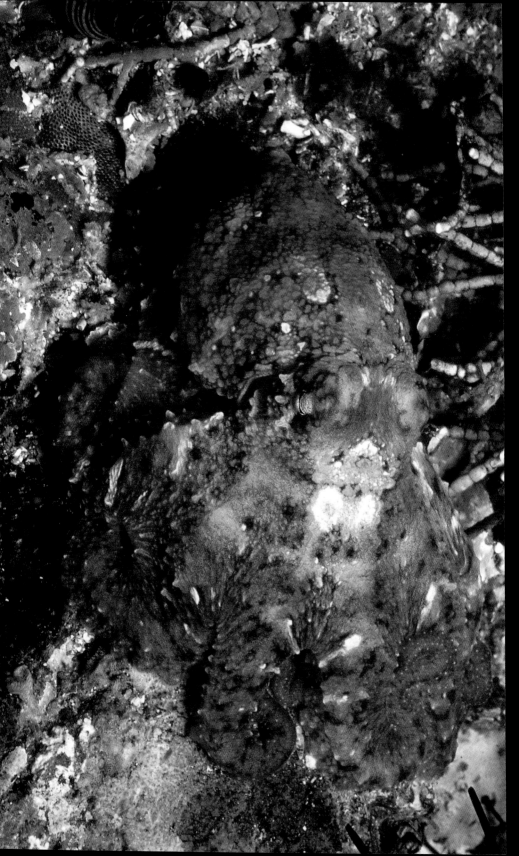

Other Cephalopods of the Pacific Coast

W hile the northeast Pacific Ocean has relatively few cephalopod species—compared to places such as Australia and the South Pacific—divers, fishers, beach walkers and boaters may encounter several species of octopuses and squids. The majority, however, live in deep water or the vast expanse of the open ocean and are seldom seen.

OCTOPUSES

Apart from the giant Pacific octopus, only one other octopus is commonly seen in relatively shallow water, the Pacific red octopus.

Pacific red octopus (ruby octopus)
Octopus rubescens

This small octopus reaches 50 cm (20 in) in radial span. It is often mistaken for a juvenile giant Pacific octopus, but the Pacific red octopus can easily be distinguished by the three tiny flaps of skin that project below each eye.

• •

Opposite: A ruby octopus displays an extraordinary repertoire of colours and textures. Photo Neil McDaniel

Top: The ultimate in recycling projects: a thumb-size ruby octopus has made a snug home out of this discarded bottle. Photo Mike Kalina

Bottom: Look carefully just below the eye of this octopus. The three tiny flaps confirm that it is a Pacific red octopus, commonly called a ruby by divers. This small species, only 50 cm across, is often observed during night dives over muddy bottoms. Photo Neil McDaniel

The Pacific red octopus ranges from Central Alaska to northern Mexico, from the shallows to a depth of at least 200 m (660 ft).

Divers usually encounter the Pacific red octopus during night dives over a mud or cobble bottom. Capable of amazing cryptic (camouflage) displays, it can blend in with various backgrounds and become nearly invisible.

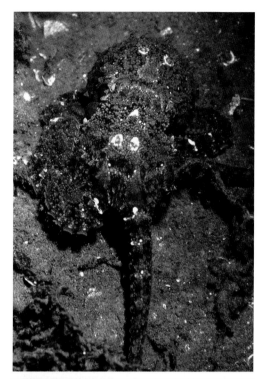

The Pacific red octopus may look puny, but it is a formidable predator, hunting mostly at night for crabs and other small prey. The octopus bites its prey and kills it with secretions from its salivary glands, then opens it at the junction between the carapace and abdomen. When annoyed this octopus may bite a human with its horny beak, and although the wound is tiny, it can be surprisingly painful (see Chapter Seven for Andy Lamb's encounter), and the effects can last for weeks.

Top: A diminutive ruby octopus on the hunt for small crabs. Note the finely pebbled texture of its skin, characteristic of this species. Photo Neil McDaniel

Bottom: Brooding Pacific red octopuses are seldom seen in the wild. The Seattle Aquarium staff provided this miniature mother with a small wooden box, and she obligingly laid a nest of eggs. Photo Leo Shaw, Seattle Aquarium

The female lays large clusters of small white eggs in rocky areas and stays to groom and protect them. The young hatch in six to eight weeks, far more quickly than the giant Pacific octopus, then spend some time in the plankton and eventually settle to the bottom.

Smoothskin octopus
Benthoctopus leioderma

Occasionally found in prawn traps, the smoothskin octopus lives in deeper water and is seldom seen. This small octopus reaches 30 cm (12 in) in radial span. It is usually found well beyond scuba diving depths, from 90 to 500 m (295 to 1,650 ft), and ranges from Siberia and northern Alaska to southern California. It is easily distinguished by its very smooth skin with a pronounced ridge along the outer sides of the mantle.

In a rare encounter, submersible pilot Jeff Heaton of Nuytco observed these octopuses during *Aquarius* dives south of Hornby Island, BC, in the summer of 1999. While the sub was sitting on the bottom at 91 m (295 ft), Jeff watched as a small smoothskin octopus emerged from a depression in the flat

mud bottom and engaged in a struggle with an unidentified prey. The octopus was only 10 cm (4 in) across. Jeff saw several during the course of the submersible dives. Other creatures observed on the muddy bottom were prawns and brittle-stars. Bottom trawls in the Strait of Georgia sometimes capture smoothskin octopuses.

With the advent of technical diving equipment and techniques, scuba divers are now exploring ever deeper water, down to 90 m (300 ft) and beyond. These adventurers may be the first to learn the secretive ways of this diminutive octopus.

Two other species of deep-water octopuses live beyond current diving depths and are almost never captured. One or more new species of octopuses are found around deep-sea hot vents and are as yet undescribed.

Above: Nuytco Research's *Aquarius,* a three-person mini-submarine, can descend to depths of about 300 m (1,000 ft). It enabled first-hand observations of smoothskin octopuses off Hornby Island in the Strait of Georgia. Photo Neil McDaniel

Opposite: Living well below conventional scuba diving depths, smoothskin octopuses appear to occupy burrows in muddy bottoms. This specimen was trawled from deep water and released in shallower water to be photographed. Photo Bernie Hanby

SQUIDS

A number of squids live in the northeast Pacific Ocean. The species most commonly seen by divers are the opalescent squid (*Loligo opalescens*) and the stubby squid (*Rossia pacifica*). Others such as the Humboldt squid (*Dosidicus gigas*), the neon flying squid (*Ommastrephes bartrami*) and the North Pacific giant squid (*Onykia robusta*, formerly known as *Moroteuthis robusta*), are occasionally caught by fishers or found stranded on beaches. BC's first documented giant squid (*Architeuthis dux*) was found washed up on Long Beach, Vancouver Island, in 2005.

Opalescent squid
Loligo opalescens

These active, fast-swimming squids have very large eyes and streamlined, torpedo-shaped bodies. When alarmed and during mating they are capable of remarkable colour displays. They have eight suckered arms plus two extensible catch tentacles with club-shaped tips. These squids reach 28 cm (11 in) long and range from southern Alaska to northern Mexico.

The adults feed on shrimp-like crustaceans, fishes and other benthic (bottom-dwelling) invertebrates. In turn they are essential food for many species of birds, fishes and marine mammals. The squids can be found in huge schools and have been the target of commercial seine fisheries off the west coast of Vancouver Island, where high-intensity lights are used to attract them to the fishing vessels. Off California they sometimes spawn in enormous aggregations composed of millions of individuals and cover hundreds of square metres of the bottom with their eggs.

Divers in BC and Washington occasionally encounter spawning masses in sheltered bays during the summer months. The squids engage in frenzied mating behaviour in which the males aggressively grab the females and deposit their sperm packet inside the mantle of the female. The females lay dozens of large cigar-shaped egg capsules, each containing 180 to 300 eggs. The newly laid eggs become attached to others, forming massive clusters that can completely cover the bottom.

Top: About 200 eggs of the opalescent squid fill each 12 cm (4.7 in) long, cigar-shaped capsule. The capsules have no taste or odour, so predators do not perceive them as food. Photo Neil McDaniel

Bottom: This mating pair of opalescent squids are not distracted even by the presence of divers. The male is below the female; when he grasps her his arms flush red, perhaps to warn off other males. Photo Neil McDaniel

175

The opalescent squid is the most commonly seen Pacific coastal species. During the summer large schools move into shallow coves and bays to mate, lay their eggs and die. Note the very large eye relative to the overall size of the squid.
Photo Neil McDaniel

The eggs develop directly and hatch in about three to five weeks, but the adults die shortly after spawning. Their carcasses attract scavengers such as bottom fishes and crabs.

Stubby squid
Rossia pacifica

These small cephalopods reach 15 cm (6 in) long. Ranging from Korea and Japan to Siberia and along the northeast Pacific coast from Alaska to northern Mexico, they are found at depths from the shallow subtidal to about 300 m (1,000 ft).

These cute little "squids" are not actually true squids, but are more closely related to cuttlefishes and commonly called bobtail squid. They have eight suckered arms and two longer tentacles as squids do, but do not have an internal quill or cuttlebone for support. They spend most of their lives on the bottom, occasionally swimming by means of their lateral fins or by jet propulsion.

Divers frequently encounter stubby squids on night dives and observe them out feeding or wandering around the bottom. During the day they usually remain partly buried in the sediment. They are quite adept at digging themselves a shallow crater in the bottom, settling in and then covering themselves with silt and sand thrown by their arms. When alarmed they can shoot out dark blobs of ink in order to distract or confuse a predator.

Female stubby squids lay up to 50 bulbous eggs, each about the size of a fingertip, usually on the underside of a rock ledge. These extremely tough egg capsules take four to nine months to hatch and receive no parental attention. The hatchlings are miniature versions of the adult and begin to attack and eat tiny prey as soon as they pop out of the egg cases.

Dr. Roland Anderson of the Seattle Aquarium, who has extensively studied this species, has found that they can be abundant in polluted urban bays such as those found throughout Puget Sound. He surmises that their short lifespan—two years—and their ability to produce a protective layer of mucous may enable them to thrive where other creatures might not. Stubby squids do well in aquaria, providing the water temperature is kept at a cold 8 to 10°C (46 to 50°F) and they are fed small live shrimp.

Top: During the day a stubby squid rests in a shallow depression it digs in the bottom. Some other species of bobtail squids have an amazing ability to disguise their silhouettes when hunting on moonlit nights. They produce light on the undersides of their body by means of a special light organ within the gill cavity that contains millions of glowing bacteria. Photo Neil McDaniel

Bottom: The female stubby squid lays up to 50 eggs, each about the size of a fingertip, on the underside of rock ledges. The eggs have extremely tough cases and hatch in four to nine months without any parental care. Photo Neil McDaniel

Top: Stubby squids are more closely related to cuttlefishes than the true squids. These cute little cephalopods are the highlight of a night dive.
Photo Neil McDaniel

Bottom: A stubby squid demonstrates a dramatic colour change by transforming from reddish brown to opalescent white in the blink of an eye.
Photo Neil McDaniel

Humboldt squid (jumbo flying squid)
Dosidicus gigas

In recent years this southern species of squid has arrived in the northeast Pacific and is easily confused with an indigenous species, the neon flying squid.

These very large, robust squids have an average mantle length of 60 cm (24 in), are 3.6 m (11.8 ft) overall and weigh up to 90 kg (200 lb). They have large diamond-shaped fins and slender, whip-like arm tips.

They are found in shallow pelagic (open ocean) habitats down to depths of several hundred metres. They usually range from Baja California and the Sea of Cortez south along the west coast of Central America to the Galapagos Islands. Large schools are found off Mexico, where they are targeted by Japanese jigging vessels that use powerful lights to attract them.

Photographer Bob Cranston shoots still photographs of a Humboldt squid in the Sea of Cortez. These powerful squids have attacked divers and are considered very dangerous when provoked by bait. Photo Howard Hall

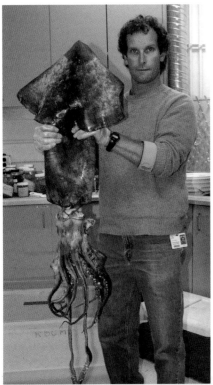

In the summer of 2004, while manager of natural history at the Royal BC Museum, Jim received some intriguing emails and phone calls. Fishers and others were catching large squids in Juan de Fuca Strait—between Vancouver Island and Washington's Olympic Peninsula—and all the way north into Alaskan waters. Finally Jim was able to get a specimen and confirm that it was a Humboldt squid. Humboldt squids have broad fins and suckers with hole saw-like rims and a unique pattern. This was the first specimen of this species ever added to the museum's collections.

• •

Top: Royal BC Museum senior collections manager Kelly Sendall displays the first specimen of a Humboldt squid documented in BC. In the fall of 2004 and subsequent years, these large and powerful predators became more common in BC. Courtesy Royal BC Museum

Bottom: In 2004 Humboldt squids invaded northeast Pacific waters. Once into the colder near-shore waters, the squids could not survive, and thousands were found washed up on beaches from Oregon to Alaska. In September 2005, campers found more than 30 on this sandy beach on Calvert Island on the central BC coast.
Photo Natasha Dickinson

• •

More sightings were soon reported by offshore survey vessels and fishers along the Oregon, Washington, BC and Alaska coasts. Unusually warm surface water temperatures as high as 19°C (66°F), several degrees higher than normal, may have influenced the movements of these large predators. During that summer an El Niño condition occurred in the northeast Pacific Ocean.

Divers who have encountered these squids report them to be aggressive and powerful, putting on amazing displays of flashing colours. In 1990, while

The rims of Humboldt squid suckers are armed with sharp teeth, making them formidable predators. This close-up is of a sucker rim about three centimetres (1.2 in) in diameter.
Courtesy Royal BC Museum

filming sequences for his award-winning PBS documentary *Shadows in a Desert Sea*, cinematographer Howard Hall and his crew got far more than they bargained for when they ventured below the surface of the Sea of Cortez at night. As Howard tells the story in *Mugged by a Squid*, "Some Mexican fishermen had been seeing big squid in the area. When asked, 'How big?' they spread their arms as wide as possible and said 'Grande!' One fisherman noticed our dive gear and asked if we intended to swim with the squid. When we said yes, he shook his head solemnly and said, 'Not a good idea.'"

Undeterred, the film crew hit the water that night. Howard recalled, "My eyes played tricks on me as I hung suspended in oppressive darkness. Startling shapes would begin to materialize and then suddenly vanish. Imagination. I wondered about what the fishermen had said. Maybe this wasn't such a good idea. I looked up toward the surface and could see the three skipjack tuna hanging over the side of the *Ambar III* for the squid to feast on should they come up. I didn't know if the squid were dangerous or not. I'd never seen a Humboldt squid. But I knew of other things that hunted in deep, dark waters that are attracted to bleeding tuna. I'd left my anti-shark suit at home in San Diego. Not a good idea at all."

When the squids finally showed up, the action got hot in a hurry. "Squid were rushing past me. Most were in the 40 or 50 pound [18 or 23 kg] class. Some approached six feet [two metres] and a hundred pounds [45 kg] or more. Something grabbed me from behind and for a moment I could feel water rushing by as I was pulled back and down. I twisted around and saw the squid that had grabbed me rush away. I'd been pulled down 10 feet [three metres]. I swam back up to 30 feet [nine metres] and neutralized my buoyancy. I didn't take the time to consider what might have happened if the squid hadn't let go, or if more than one had grabbed me, or if a really big one had . . . "

In the end the crew got the shots they wanted for the film, along with a blast of adrenalin!

Neon flying squid
Ommastrephes bartrami

Neon flying squids belong to the same family as Humboldt squids and are very similar in many of their external features. They are indigenous to the waters of the North Pacific, Atlantic and Indian oceans. Confusion between neon flying squids and Humboldt squids has led some fishers to believe that Humboldt squids have been in northern waters for many years.

Neon flying squids spend their summers (July through September) in northern waters and then migrate to subtropical waters in the winter. They also spawn in warmer southern waters.

These squids are very short-lived, like most cephalopods, and are thought to survive for only a year. Females grow to about 60 cm (2 ft) in dorsal mantle length and about 5.3 kg (12 lb) in weight. Males are slightly smaller and lighter.

Neon flying squids consume small fishes, other squids (including each other), and planktonic organisms such as euphausids. In turn the squids serve as prey for swordfishes, marlins, sharks, tunas, marine mammals and sea birds.

An easy way to tell the difference between Humboldt squids and neon flying squids is to examine the toothed sucker rims. Neon flying squids have four cardinal teeth in the north, south,

Neon flying squids and Humboldt squids look remarkably similar, but the position of the teeth on their sucker rims makes it possible to tell them apart. A neon squid sucker rim has four larger teeth 90 degrees apart, while the Humboldt squid has small teeth on one side of the rim progressing to larger teeth on the other. This close-up photo shows a neon squid sucker rim about two centimetres (0.8 in) in diameter. Courtesy Royal BC Museum

east and west positions. Humboldt squids have teeth progressing in size from very small to a few much larger teeth on one side of the rim.

North Pacific giant squid
Onykia robusta (formerly known as *Moroteuthis robusta*)

These massive squids reach 3.4 m (11 ft) long. When the tentacles are included in the measurement, they can reach up to seven metres (23 ft) in overall length. They range widely throughout the Atlantic Ocean, Indian Ocean, Japan and Siberia, and from northern Alaska to southern California. They are pelagic, living from the surface to depths of 600 m (2,000 ft).

Top: In this rare image, a photographer encounters a North Pacific giant squid near the coast of Japan. Distressed and dying animals are sometimes found in shallow water. Photo Katsunori Seki

Bottom: Emily Mulleda and Robin Pozer were out digging razor clams on North Beach, Queen Charlotte Islands, when they discovered a stranded North Pacific giant squid. Emily convinced her husband Norman Deering to take home a piece and fry it, but "it tasted terrible—very bitter and salty." Photo Norman Deering

Adults are easily identified by the 15 to 18 pairs of claw-like hooks on the feeding tentacle clubs.

Onykia are occasionally observed swimming at the surface well out to sea or found washed up dead on the beach. They are commonly caught by fishers trapping sablefish (Alaska black cod) in waters exceeding 300 m (1,000 ft) deep. In the northern Pacific Ocean *Onykia* are a significant prey item for sperm whales.

Giant squid

Architeuthis dux

These deep-ocean squids grow to tremendous size. The females reach 13 m (43 ft) long, including the two long catch tentacles; the males reach 10 m (33 ft) long. This makes these squids the second largest mollusc in the world, second only to colossal squids (*Mesonychoteuthis hamiltoni*), which reach 14 m (46 ft) overall and have a mantle nearly twice as long as giant squids.

Giant squids feed on deep-sea fishes, and remote video taken by Japanese researchers in 2004 shows them to be aggressive, powerful predators. In turn giant squids are the favoured prey of sperm whales, which are capable of remarkably deep and lengthy dives. Captured sperm whales are often covered with sucker marks from giant squids, presumably received during their deep-sea battles.

Recovered specimens show that giant squids are widespread and occur in all of the world's oceans. In the North Atlantic they are especially abundant in the waters around Norway, Newfoundland and the northern British Isles. In the South Atlantic they have been reported off the coast of Africa. In the Pacific Ocean they are known from the waters off New Zealand, where there is a large population of sperm whales, and Japan.

Giant squids are apparently rare in the northeast Pacific Ocean, but in the summer of 2005 the remains of a massive squid were found on Long Beach in Pacific Rim National Park on the west coast of Vancouver Island. Parks Canada staff collected and froze the specimen, which was eventually transported to the Royal BC Museum in Victoria and identified as a giant squid. This was the first and still the only record of the giant squid in BC.

A necropsy of the specimen revealed that it had been attacked by a sperm whale, which left a distinct line of tooth holes in the mantle.

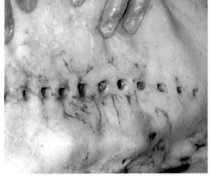

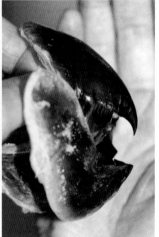

Top: This giant squid, the first documented in BC, was found August 11, 2005, on Long Beach on Vancouver Island by Parks Canada staff. The immature female was killed by a sperm whale. Photo Heather Holmes

Above left: A line of tooth punctures made in the mantle of this giant squid were the result of a fatal encounter with a sperm whale (*Physeter catadon*). Photo Jim Cosgrove

Above right: The razor-sharp beak of the giant squid is a fearsome weapon. The stomachs of sperm whales sometimes contain hundreds of these beaks. Photo Jim Cosgrove

OTHER CEPHALOPODS

Other cephalopods found in the North Pacific are listed only by order, suborder, family and scientific name. Many do not have common names, and information about most of the deep-water species is very sparse.

Order Teuthoidea
Suborder Oegopsida

Family Enoploteuthidae
Abraliopsis felis

Family Octopoteuthidae
Octopoteuthis deletron

Family Onychoteuthidae
Onychoteuthis borealijaponica

Family Gonatidae
Berryteuthis anonychus
Berryteuthis magister
Gonatopsis borealis
Gonatus berryi
Gonatus californiensis
Gonatus madokai
Gonatus onyx
Gonatus oregonensis
Gonatus pyros
Gonatus ursabrunae

Family Histioteuthidae
Histioteuthis dofleini

Family Ommastrephidae
Todarodes pacificus

Family Chiroteuthidae
Chiroteuthis calyx
Planctoteuthis oligobessa

Family Cranchiidae
Cranchia scabra
Galiteuthis phyllura
Leachia dislocata
Taonius pavo

Order Vampyromorpha

Family Vampyroteuthidae
Vampyroteuthis infernalis

Order Octopoda
Suborder Cirrata

Family Cirroteuthidae
Cirroteuthis muelleri

Family Opisthoteuthidae
Opisthoteuthis californiana

Suborder Incirrata

Family Bolitaenidae
Japatella diaphana

Family Octopodidae
Benthoctopus abruptus
Benthoctopus profundum

Glossary

Ammonite: A type of ancient cephalopod with a rigid, often spiral-shaped external shell, which lived in the oceans between 400 and 65 million years ago (mya). It became extinct around the same time as the dinosaurs.

Apex species: A food web or food chain begins with the producers (plants or animals that use sunlight and carbon dioxide or some form of chemical energy), and continues through various levels of consumers to one or more apex species. A natural death for all plants and animals is to be eaten by something else. Only an apex species is expected to die of old age. A sperm whale is an example of an apex species.

Belemnite: A type of ancient cephalopod that looked somewhat squid-like, with paired fins and an internal chambered shell. It became extinct around 65 mya.

Benthic: Refers to organisms that live on or in the bottom of an ocean or lake.

Bilateral symmetry: A type of body arrangement in which the left and right sides are mirror images.

Branchial heart: The octopus has two branchial hearts, one at the base of each gill. They function to pump blood to the main heart (somatic heart).

Camouflage: The use of colour, texture and shape to disguise a creature's presence.

Cannibalism: Predation in which an animal eats members of its own species.

Carnivore: An organism that feeds on flesh or other animal matter.

Cephalopod: A Greek term meaning "head-foot." Members of the class Cephalopoda are the living forms and include the Nautiloids (see **Nautilus**), the Sepids (see **Cuttlefish**), the Teuthoids (see **Squid**) and the Octopods (see **Octopus**) as well as a number of smaller groups.

Cephalotoxin: A toxin produced by cephalopods such as octopuses and squids. In certain species such as the blue-ringed octopuses, this toxin can be deadly to humans.

Chemotactic: Sensing chemicals by touching.

Chitinous: Formed of horny material, e.g. the shell of a crab or the beak of an octopus.

Chiton: A type of bottom-dwelling mollusc with eight individual shell plates; usually herbivorous.

Chromatophores: Pigment-containing and light-reflecting cells found in amphibians, fishes, reptiles, crustaceans and cephalopods. They are responsible for generating skin and eye colour.

Copepod: A small aquatic crustacean. Most species are barely visible to the unaided eye.

Cryptic: Having colouration or texture that serves to conceal.

Ctenidia: A gill; a comb-like organ used by an aquatic organism to absorb oxygen from water.

Ctenophore: A gelatinous, planktonic marine animal with swimming organs called comb rows; commonly known as a comb jelly.

Cuttlefish: A cephalopod characterized by having a short body with lateral fins, eight arms, two tentacles and an internal calcareous shell.

Ectoparasite: A plant or animal living on the outside surface of another and drawing nutriment from its host.

El Niño: An abnormal warming of surface ocean waters in the eastern tropical Pacific Ocean. It can result in subtropical marine species temporarily extending their range farther north along the Pacific coast of North America.

Endoparasite: A plant or animal living inside another and drawing nutriment from its host.

Esophagus: In the octopus, a short tube through which food passes to the crop.

Extensible: Refers to an organ that can extend or stretch out, such as the extensible tentacles of squids and cuttlefishes.

Extinction: The dying out of an entire species.

Extirpation: The total eradication of a species from a specific area while it survives in other areas.

Hectocotylus: Refers to the distal end of the third right arm of the male octopus, which does not have suckers running its entire length. Instead the end of that arm has a groove that is used to hold and transfer the sperm packet into the mantle cavity of the female.

Hemocyanin: An oxygen-carrying substance containing copper, present in the blood plasma of molluscs and arthropods.

Hemoglobin: An oxygen-carrying substance containing iron, present in the red blood cells of vertebrate animals.

Indigenous: Plants and animals occurring naturally within a given geographic region.

Innate: A response or action that is inborn and not learned.

Interbrachial web: The thin web of skin that stretches between the arms of an octopus, which uses it to envelop and hold prey.

Invertebrate: An animal that lacks a true backbone.

Iridophores: Pigment cells containing tiny plates that reflect light.

Leucophores: Pigment cells containing tiny plates that refract (bend) light.

Midden: The remains of meals (crab shells, clam shells, etc.) that are deposited in front of an octopus den.

MYA (mya): An abbreviation for millions of years ago.

Mysid: A type of shrimp-like planktonic crustacean that often forms huge swarms.

Nautilus: A cephalopod with an external shell that belongs to the subclass Nautiloidea. It is among the most primitive of the living cephalopods.

Nekton: Any animal that can steadily swim against a one-knot current.

Nudibranch: A member of the phylum Mollusca and a relative of the cephalopods. Nudibranchs have lost their shells in the process of evolution. The word "nudibranch" means "naked gills." Commonly referred to as a sea slug.

Octopus: Most members of the order Octopoda have eight arms and no tentacles. Octopuses are solitary, except when mating, and short-lived. With few exceptions octopuses are benthic (bottom-dwelling) as adults.

Oviduct: A tube leading from the ovary to the mantle cavity of a female octopus. Eggs produced in the ovaries are fertilized as they pass down the oviducts. Sperm are deposited in the oviducts by the male(s).

Paralarvae: Developing octopuses do not go through different larval stages like those found in crustaceans such as crabs. Instead they develop from an egg directly into a miniature of the adult at hatching, and the offspring are termed paralarvae.

Pelagic: Derived from a Greek word meaning "open ocean;" any water away from the bottom.

Phytoplankton: Plants that drift in the water—either salt water or fresh water—and are not attached to the bottom.

Plankton: Any plant or animal that drifts with the water currents and cannot swim against a one-knot current (see **Nekton**).

Protozoa: Means "first animals" in Greek. The kingdom Protista contains many unicellular organisms such as amoebae. Most protozoans are microscopic, and many cause diseases.

Radial span: A measure of an octopus across the width of the animal, as if you were measuring the diameter of an open umbrella.

Radula: A file-like rasping structure found in the mouth of many molluscs. Consisting of pointed teeth on a ribbon-like base, the radula is used to tear food into small bits or to drill holes in the shells of prey.

SEM: The Scanning Electron Microscope produces images of a sample by scanning it with a high-energy beam of electrons. It produces images of very high magnification, up to 250 times greater than the best light microscopes. A SEM has an extremely large depth of field, which yields a characteristic and extremely detailed three-dimensional appearance.

Senescent: Refers to an animal nearing the end of its life in old age. Giant Pacific octopuses sometimes exhibit strange behaviour when senescent.

Siphonophore: A pelagic (open ocean) animal related to sea jellies and sea anemones. Siphonophores commonly have powerful stings; the best known of these is the Portuguese man-of-war.

Somatic heart: One of three hearts in an octopus. This heart circulates the blood from the gills to the body and back to the two branchial hearts (see **Branchial heart**).

Spermatophore: A tubular structure that contains the sperm of the male cephalopod, generally passed to the female during mating. A specialized arm on the male (see **Hectocotylus**) is used to transfer the spermatophore.

Squid: Most members of the order Teuthoidea are decapods with eight arms and two tentacles. Squids are free-swimming and often travel together in large numbers. The colossal squid and the giant squid are the largest invertebrate animals in the world.

Tentacles: The two extensible modified arms of decapods such as squids and cuttlefishes. The tentacles commonly have large arrays of suckers on the ends (see **Tentacular club**) that are used to catch and secure food. All the undifferentiated arms of the nautilus are also termed tentacles, but they are not the same as those of the squids and cuttlefishes.

Tentacular club: At the end of each of the two tentacles of a squid or cuttlefish is a broad pad of suckers. Often the suckers have toothed rims or hooks or both. These structures allow the capture of fast-swimming prey such as fishes.

Total length: The measure of an animal from the tip of the head to the tip of the foot. In the case of a cephalopod, this is from the tip of the mantle to the tip of the longest arm or tentacle.

Water column: The conceptual body of water surrounding an organism in which it lives and moves. The water column extends from the surface to the bottom and has no limit on how wide it can be.

Zooplankton: The animal portion of the plankton, which drifts with the currents and is unable to swim against a one-knot current. Zooplankton are usually larger than the plant portion of the plankton (see **Phytoplankton**) and commonly feed on the plants.

Bibliography

Akimushkin, I.I. *Octopus dofleini* (Wülker, 1910). In: Cephalopods of the Seas of the USSR, 1963.

Allemandy, Victor. *Wonders of the Deep: The Story of the Williamson Submarine Expedition.* London: Jarrold & Sons, 1915.

Anderson, R.C. "How smart are octopuses?" *Coral* 2, no. 1 (2005): 44–48.

Anderson, R.C., R. Shimek, J.A. Cosgrove and S. Berthiner. "Giant Pacific octopus, *Enteroctopus dofleini,* attacks on divers." *Canadian Field-Naturalist* (forthcoming).

Cerullo, Mary M. *The Octopus: Phantom of the Sea.* New York: Cobblehill Books, 1997.

Cosgrove, J.A. "An in situ observation of webover hunting by the giant Pacific octopus, *Enteroctopus dofleini* (Wülker, 1910)." *The Canadian Field-Naturalist* 117 (2002): 117–18.

Cosgrove, J.A. *In situ* observations of nesting female *Octopus dofleini. Journal of Cephalopod Biology,* Vol. 2(2) (1993): 33–46.

Cosgrove, J.A. The first specimens of Humboldt squid in British Columbia. Pisces Press. Vol. 13, No. 2 (2005): 30–31.

Cosgrove, J.A., and K.A. Sendall. "Notes on the first giant squid, *Architeuthis dux* (Steenstrup, 1857), found in British Columbia, Canada." Victoria: BC Archives, 2007. http://www.bcarchives.bc.ca/Content_Files/Files/collections%20and%20research/Natural%20History/ReportfirstPacificGiantSquid.pdf

Cousteau, J.Y., and P. Diole. *Octopus and Squid: The Soft Intelligence.* Garden City, NY: Doubleday, 1973.

Dall, W.H. "Aleutian cephalopods." *American Naturalist* 7 (1873): 484–85.

Dall, W.H. "The arms of the octopus, or devil fish." *Science* 6, no. 145 (1885): 432.

Ellis, David W., and Luke Swan. *Teachings of the Tides: Uses of the Marine Invertebrates by the Manhousat People.* Nanaimo, BC: Theytus Books, 1981.

Ellis, Richard. *Monsters of the Sea.* Guilford, CT: The Lyons Press, 2006.

Gabe, S.H. Reproduction in the giant octopus of the North Pacific, *Octopus dofleini martini. The Veliger,* Vol. 18, No. 2 (1975): 146-150.

Gillespie, G.E., G. Parker and J. Morrison. *Fisheries biology of the giant Pacific octopus (Octopus dofleini) (Wulker, 1910), with a discussion of octopus fisheries in British Columbia.* Canadian Stock Assessment Secretariat Research Document 98/87. Ottawa: Fisheries and Oceans Canada, 1998.

Guinness World Records 2008. London: Guinness Publishing, 2008.

Hanlon, R.T., and J.B. Messenger. 1996. *Cephalopod Behaviour.* Cambridge: Cambridge University Press, 1996.

Hartwick, E.B., L. Tulloch and S. Macdonald. Feeding and growth of *Octopus dofleini* (Wülker). *The Veliger,* Vol. 24, No. 2 (1981): 129–138.

Hochberg, F.G., and W.G. Fields. "Cephalopoda: The squids and octopuses." In *Intertidal Invertebrates of California,* edited by R.H. Morris, D.P. Abbott and E.C. Haderlie, 429–44. Stanford: Stanford University Press, 1980.

Hugo, Victor. *Toilers of the Sea.* Paris: 1866. Quoted in Richard Ellis, *Monsters of the Sea* (Guilford, CT: The Lyons Press, 2006).

Hunt, J.C. *Octopus and Squid.* Monterey Bay Aquarium Natural History Series. Monterey Bay, CA: Monarch Books, 1996.

Knappert, Jan. *Pacific Mythology: An Encyclopedia of Myth and Legend.* London: Diamond Books, 1995.

Lamb, Andy, and Bernard Hanby. *Marine Life of the Pacific Northwest: A Photographic Encyclopedia.* Madeira Park, BC: Harbour Publishing, 2005.

Lane, Frank W. *Kingdom of the Octopus.* New York: Pyramid, 1960.

Linden, Eugene. *The Octopus and the Orangutan: More True Tales of Animal Intrigue, Intelligence, and Ingenuity.* Toronto: Penguin Books, 2002.

Mather, J.A., and R.C. Anderson. "Personalities of octopus." *Journal of Comparative Psychology* 107 (1993): 336–40.

Mather, J.A., and R.C. Anderson. "What behavior can we expect of octopuses?" Halifax: The Cephalopod Page, 1998. http://www.thecephalopodpage.org/behavior.php

Mather, J.A. "How do octopuses use their arms?" *Journal of Comparative Psychology* 112 (1998): 306–18.

Mather, J.A., and R.C. Anderson. "Octopuses are smart suckers!" Halifax: The Cephalopod Page, 2000. http://www.the-cephalopodpage.org/smarts.php

Mather, J.A., S. Resler and J.A. Cosgrove. Activity and Movement patterns of *Octopus dofleini. Journal of Marine Behaviour and Physiology*, Vol. 11 (1985): 301–14.

Morris, R.H., D.P. Abbott and E.C. Haderlie. *Intertidal Invertebrates of California.* Stanford: Stanford University Press, 1980.

Nesis, K.N. *Cephalopods of the World.* Neptune, NJ: T.F.H. Publications, 1987.

Newman, Murray. *Life in a Fishbowl: Confessions of an Aquarium Director.* Vancouver: Douglas & McIntyre, 1994.

Nixon, Marion, and John Z. Young. *The Brains and Lives of Cephalopods.* Oxford: Oxford University Press, 2003.

Norman, Mark. *Cephalopods: A World Guide.* Hackenheim, Germany: ConchBooks, 2002.

Pliny the Elder. *Naturalis Historia.* Loeb Classical Library. Harvard: Harvard University Press, 1933.

Shearar, Cheryl. *Understanding Northwest Coast Art.* Vancouver: Douglas & McIntyre, 2000.

Sheel, D. Characteristics of habitats used by *Enteroctopus dofleini* in Prince William Sound and Cook Inlet, Alaska. P.S.Z.N.: *Marine Ecology*, Vol. 23(3) (2002): 185–206.

Soule, Gardner, ed. *Under the Sea: A Treasury of Great Writing about the Ocean Depths.* New York: Meredith Press, 1968.

Stewart, Hilary. *Indian Fishing: Early Methods on the Northwest Coast.* Vancouver: Douglas & McIntyre, 1997.

Williams, G., Lieut.-Commander, RN. *Diving for Treasure and Other Adventures Beneath the Sea.* London: Faber and Gwyer, 1926.

Williamson, J.E. *Twenty Years Under the Sea.* Boston: Hale, Cushman and Flint, 1936.

Acknowledgements

Jim Cosgrove would like to acknowledge the hundreds of divers who braved the chilly waters around Victoria to assist in his octopus research over the years. They are too numerous to name individually, but the assistance of each and every one was greatly appreciated. There are a few especially dedicated people who deserve recognition, including Michael Barber, Jeannie Cosgrove, David Gagliardi, Jim Mendria, David Pickles, Leah Saville and Kevin Van Cleemput.

Jim would like to thank Dr. Jennifer Mather, who set him on the path of formal research on octopuses; Dr. Jack Littlepage, his supervisor during his M.Sc. research at the University of Victoria; Mrs. Ruby Littlepage for her years of encouragement and support; Dr. Brian Hartwick, a leader in giant Pacific octopus research on the West Coast and one of the founding members of the Canadian Association for Underwater Science; and Dr. Henry Reiswig, who made superb high-resolution images of giant Pacific octopus radulas.

Dr. Roland Anderson of the Seattle Aquarium, Dr. David Sheel of the University of Alaska and Dr. Eric Hochberg of Santa Barbara Museum of Natural History are thanked for their enthusiastic willingness to discuss Pacific octopuses and to share their photographs and research findings.

Jim would also like to acknowledge Fisheries and Oceans Canada and the Institute of Ocean Sciences for permitting access to the boat launch ramp at Patricia Bay; the staff of the Biology Department of Camosun College; the executive of the Royal BC Museum for their support of his research; and the southern Vancouver Island branch of BC Parks for permitting vehicle access to Gowlland-Tod Park; and NHK Japan for allowing access to their video footage of nesting giant Pacific octopuses.

One final acknowledgement is to Nicholas McClusky of Manheim, Pennsylvania, who as a six-year-old sent Jim $20 of his Christmas money. He sent his gift because he saw a documentary about Jim's work on TV and wanted to support his research.

Neil McDaniel would like to thank the many dive buddies who have shared the enjoyment over the years. He managed to maintain a dive log, so his failing memory has a reliable backup. Special thanks are due to Kevin Van Cleemput, Fred Demchuk, Geoff Grognet, Doug Swanston, Andy Lamb, Randy Haight, Donnie Reid, Gary Bridges, Lou Lehmann, Mark Atherton and Jeff Heaton who have provided assistance in obtaining octopus photographs and first-hand observations.

Neil would also like to acknowledge fellow underwater photographers Fred Bavendam, David Fleetham, Brandon Cole, Doug Pemberton, Bernie Hanby, Rick Harbo, Jim Willoughby, Howard Hall and Mike Kalina for contributing their exceptional and often rare images. Fred Bavendam was especially generous in giving the authors access to his comprehensive library of octopus images. Thanks, too, to Mark Hobson of Tofino, for the use of his dramatic watercolour *King of the Kelp Forest* and to fellow artists Patrick Amos, Glen Rabena, Mark Henderson and Bill Henderson.

Jim and Neil would also like to thank Adrienne Aikins for her original drawings and several other individuals who generously shared their fascinating observations and exceptional photographs. These include Heather Bates-White, Brady Bell, Philip Bruecker, Pete Brown, Don Coleman, Norman Deering, Natasha Dickinson, Graham Gillespie, Kevin Harman, Noel Hendrickson, Bill High, Vallorie Hodges, Heather Holmes, Danny Kent, Cliff Law, Peter Luckham, John McGuire, Sandy Matheson, Danny Mauro, Emily Mulleda, Sandra Palm, Robin Pozer, Katsunori Seki, Leo Shaw, Anne Sheridan and Susan Snyder. Thanks as well to David W. Ellis and James Swan for kindly permitting the use of "The Legend of Mr. Raven and Miss Octopus" in chapter one.

Our book profited greatly from the eagle-eyed ministrations of Susan Mayse, who had the daunting task of editing our manuscript. Thank you, Susan.

Our sincere thanks to designer Martin Nichols, who worked wonders with our disorganized pile of photographs and reams of text.

And lastly, we must express our gratitude to Harbour's Production Manager Anna Comfort, who dealt so patiently with our blizzard of e-mails, keeping this project on the rails and headed in the right direction at all times.

About the Authors

JAMES COSGROVE

Jim began scuba diving in 1959 in Nova Scotia. After moving to BC, he became a display diver and specimen collector at the Pacific Undersea Gardens in Victoria. During his early diving career he had many unforgettable encounters with the giant Pacific octopus, and while at the University of Victoria, he devoted his master's thesis to the study of aspects of its natural history. Since then he has continued his research, publishing scientific papers on various aspects of its biology.

Jim is a founding member of the Canadian Association for Underwater Science (CAUS) and served for 30 years as the diving safety officer for the University of Victoria. He has also provided his expertise to documentary film crews from around the globe. Jim is now recognized as a world expert on the giant Pacific octopus. In 2007 he retired from his position as manager of the natural history section at the Royal BC Museum. (Photo Jeannie Cosgrove)

NEIL McDANIEL

Neil has been photographing marine life since 1969, when he learned to scuba dive while completing a degree in marine zoology at the University of British Columbia. After graduation, he worked as an ecology technician at the Pacific Environment Institute in West Vancouver and later became the editor of *DIVER* magazine. He has written and illustrated many articles for international wildlife magazines and contributed to many books. Neil has an avid ongoing interest in the natural history of BC's coastal marine life and currently works as a freelance photographer and cinematographer, primarily on nature documentaries. (Photo Geoff Grognet)

Index

Bold entries indicate a photograph or illustration.